Created in Her Image

Created in Her Image

Models of the Feminine Divine

Eleanor Rae

and

Bernice Marie-Daly

CROSSROAD · NEW YORK

1990

The Crossroad Publishing Company
370 Lexington Avenue
New York, NY 10017

Printed in the United States of America

Library of Congress Cataloging-in-Publication Data

Rae, Eleanor.
    Created in her image : models of the feminine divine / Eleanor
Rae, Bernice Marie-Daly.
        p.   cm.
    Includes bibliographical references.
    ISBN 0-8245-1013-5
    1. Femininity of God.   I. Marie-Daly, Bernice.   II. Title.
BT153.M6R34   1990
231'.4—dc20   89-48898
                                                            CIP

To my mother,
Clare Marie Cawley,

and to all our mothers,
mothers, mothers, mothers . . .

Bernice Marie-Daly

To the two realities that are part of my life as I write: the cutting of the forests and the singing of the birds; the cutting (of the forests) and the singing (of the birds); the cutting and the singing. Do we not know, if we have only the cutting, we will no longer have the singing?

Eleanor Rae

Contents

Acknowledgments

As one goes through life, whatever the paths one chooses, the realization deepens that one is a part of the larger process: both human and divine.

Some of the family members who have been a particular part of my book-writing process at this time are my husband, Giles, who has shared the joys and pains of a first-time author; my children, Cynthia, Robert, Susan, Michael, Giles, and Karen, who always welcomed my loving if sometimes limited presence; my grandchildren, Ian, Hawley, and Sara, who are my vision concretized; my father, John, who personified unconditional love; and my mother, Eva Stella, who gave me her gifts of prophecy, theology, and courage. Outside of my family, I am particularly indebted to Bernice Marie-Daly, who enthusiastically joined her path with mine for this book-writing adventure; Carol M. Lisi, whose drawing of the birthing Spirit, as well as whose friendship, said, The pain is worth the goal; Paula Hand, who graciously tailored her typing assignments to my jagged schedule; the Ridgefield Connecticut Public Library, which found me so many hard-to-locate source materials; and the Holy Spirit, who found the ones the Ridgefield Library could not find, and whose continued presence to me is my greatest joy and reason for being.

—Eleanor Rae

Acknowledgments

A book, like everything else, is not created in a vacuum. There are probably more people and energies that have contributed to these pages than I can know. Nonetheless, I first want to acknowledge my family: my husband, John, for his support and encouragement; my children, Deirdre and Jay, for their questions and concerns as well as the hope they offer for the future. Second, my "family of origin," which molded my initial views and perceptions: my mother, Clare Marie Cawley, who has offered much to me, not least of which is an image of what it means to be a strong woman; my father, John Jerome Cawley, who in his absence spoke volumes; my brother Paul, who has spent most of his life helping others; my sister Mary, who has been immeasurably devoted to the family and who helped me in my growing-up years; my sister Annmarie, who has been supportive of me throughout this project; and Clare, a special sister-friend, with whom I have shared much of my journey.

I am grateful for the suggestions and support of many friends, associates, and colleagues who have assisted me in diverse and mysterious ways, especially: Christina del Piero, Skip Vilas, and of course Eleanor Rae, as well as my publisher and editors. I am particularly indebted and grateful for the friendship, talent, and enthusiastic discussions I have enjoyed with Midge Miles. I would like to thank Maria Harris for her affirmation and her overall comments and critique; Donna Wilshire for her enthusiasm and suggestions on The Goddess; and the staff of the New Canaan Library's interlibrary loan department, who greatly assisted my research efforts.

—Bernice Marie-Daly

Introduction

This book is the meeting, joining, and interweaving of two journeys. For me it began in a need to find a suitable pronoun with which to refer to the Holy Spirit. For Bernice, it began as a need to respond to an image. Synchronistically, we each discovered the image of a mosaic as a symbol of the weaving together of our two perspectives.

While writing my dissertation on the Holy Spirit, I was faced with the need to find a suitable pronoun to use when referring to the Spirit. Although the creeds and contemporary theologies use the pronoun *He*, my experience of the Holy Spirit was not that of a masculine presence; for me to refer to the Holy Spirit as *He* would have been a negation of my own religious experience. Should I then, I asked myself, be true to my experience and speak of the Spirit in feminine terms? I was not aware of any place in the tradition where the Spirit was addressed as the feminine aspect of God. I was hesitant to take this radical step. Therefore I uncomfortably settled on using *it* to refer to the Spirit, with the promise to myself that, as soon as my dissertation was completed, I would go back to investigate the tradition to see whether there were any portions of it that resonated to my experience of the Holy Spirit as God's feminine presence.

I found that my experience was not unique. In my speaking engagements I shared my knowledge with others. The response was quite powerful: often positive, sometimes negative, but never lukewarm. In time I had enough material for a book and began to write it. But time for writing was very limited. It was then that I met Bernice, who was also coming from a strong religious experience.

For me, Bernice, the inner image that gestated these pages was a caldron. My body/spirit psychic sense carries this caldron—a huge black pot simmering with the varied and intense fragments of my soul, making a grand "potluck." All of my significant pieces bubble here, adding new insights and concerns. The intensity gurgles and causes inner upheavals and volcanic eruptions. Eventually I began to realize that I had to put these energies to good use or I would be consumed! And so I began. These writings attempt to articulate what has been "stewing

1

around inside of me" related to the need to search for a sacred image that affirms femaleness—women's psycho-spiritual growth as well as some of my personal experiences of the numinous. The more I honor my own inner juices—the more I consistently say out loud, in my own voice, what I need to say—the more the volcanic eruptions subside.

In the midst of ruminating on these pages, I had a dream. I was deep within the earth, in the inner recesses of a cave, standing in a circle with many others, dressed in a long cream-white robe. In the center was a large black caldron with a fire underneath. A ceremony was taking place. It involved the silent, awesome, passing of a sacred object from person to person. As it was passed to me, I realized it was a child wrapped as a papoose. The child somehow came from the caldron and was a Divine Child. After dialoguing with this image, I came to know Her as my Inner Child, my Inner Wisdom Child. This book is part of Her Inner Wisdom.

There remains our common image of a mosaic. This mosaic—the continuing consciousness raising of the women's movement, the scholarship of feminist theologians, the resurgence of the feminine as understood psychologically, the "new age," ecological realities, the popularity of religious fundamentalism, new scientific insights, national and international economic and political crises, threats of nuclear disasters, and more—forms a grand design representing the uniqueness of our age, which requires the birthing of a new vision for ourselves, our relationships, our planet. We became increasingly aware of our need to contribute to that mosaic: to place our tiny piece of colored glass—our perspective, energy, and commitment—carefully among the many other small pieces of colored glass so that together the brilliance, splendor, and wisdom of a new story may be told. We are convinced that the return of the feminine Divine is an absolutely essential and primary condition for this telling.

Why This Is a Critical Issue

This book represents our discoveries, many of which lie within the structures of our Judeo-Christian tradition. We have limited our discussion to the Western world, which in no way negates the richness of experience that exists in the East (a second volume could present these experiences.) But, within the Western milieu, we have not limited ourselves exclusively to Judeo-Christianity. Rather, we have tried to enter into dialogue with those who came before us who worshiped the Goddess, as well as those, presently in our midst, who experience Her as the source of all.[1] We realize that this will make us suspect in the eyes of some, but, in an age that has witnessed the gathering of all the great patriarchal religions for prayer, we believe strongly that the great matriarchal tradition must also be included. We do this with the understanding that "the truth of the mystery of God and the liberation of human beings grow in direct and not inverse proportion."[2]

Further, we are aware that such an inclusion of the feminine Divine will ultimately mean that nothing will remain unchanged. This is precisely the scope of the change for which the earth and its creatures are crying out. But once this need is recognized (and each day more people are recognizing that we are living in a world where death, not life, is ultimately worshiped), we are faced with the question of the appropriate response. Some have responded through actions, and that is a necessary part of the response. For unless we are willing to go out and co-create with Her, there will never be a new world. Others have responded with ideas, prayers, and vision, and that is also part of the response. For if we do not have the image of the new world before us, we will not have the power to bring it into being. Ultimately, the active and the contemplative are merely the mirror images of one unity, for the vision empowers the action while the action enables the vision both to become a reality and to evolve.

We see the kind of power and enablement that is needed today in the image of the feminine Divine. For if the earth is to be saved, we must all practice the "feminine" virtues of compassion, nurturance, wisdom, interdependence, strength, and inner truth, and relinquish the attitudes that stand for "power over." While men must, and, in fact, are already, imagining the feminine Divine,[3] it is precisely the half of the human race now in bondage that must free itself to image Her reality. For while it may still be true "that to be human is to be male is to be the Son of God,"[4] we are proposing a reversal of this equation whereby women will experience that to be human is, for them, to be female, is to be the Daughter of Goddess. For a woman to accept the Divine Person as male can bring no other consequences than the destruction of her own personhood.[5] This destruction has in fact been experienced in the reality we call sexism.

Sexism is the elementary human sin because it perverts the basic human female/male dyad. One part of the human dyad (the female) has been perverted and, as such, all humanity is perverted. The deformation of the female and feminine experience is the first stumbling block we encounter in our culture and it invites all oppression. "Power over," frequently associated with money or might or both, is seen as normative for "human" behavior.[6] Domination/subjugation becomes the norm for sexism, racism, ageism, militarism, elitism, classism, and so forth. The feminist agenda, therefore, is "integral to any humanism and any ethics, since it addresses the foundational crisis of the corrective perversion of the male/female human."[7] And it is equally significant to the future development among species since it is unlikely that there will be respect for the air, water, fish, or trees when there is still little respect for the primary human dyad. Thus, critical issues hinge on the fact that we have allowed ourselves to image only a male god. Sexism has now spilled over into ecological planetary disaster.

Yet there is no reason for women (or men) to believe that the norm for humanity ought to be based solely on a maleness that resides in the Divinity. Rather, as our Scripture acknowledges in the first chapter of the first book, when God creates in God's own image, God creates both male and female (Gen. 1:27). "If this is true, then there must be in God, in a transcendent form, something that corresponds to masculinity and something that corresponds to femininity."[8] The chapters in this book will explore "that which corresponds to femininity." However, before we outline the contents of these chapters, it is necessary to look at the issues of language and of the meaning of religion as a symbol system.

Language

That the Judeo-Christian tradition, as well as the wider societal structure, has supported the oppression of women, is poignantly evidenced by the development of a patriarchal culture. A powerful contemporary metaphor for women's struggle against this oppression is the metaphor of finding one's voice, of the power of language.

> In describing their lives, women commonly [talk] about voice and silence: "speaking up," "speaking out," "being silenced," "not being heard," "really listening," "really talking," "words as weapons," "feeling deaf and dumb," "having no words," and so on in an endless variety of connotations all having to do with sense of mind, self-worth, and feelings of isolation from or connection to others. . . . Women repeatedly [use] the metaphor of voice to depict their intellectual and ethical development; and that the development of a sense of voice, mind, and self [are] intricately intertwined.[9]

Maria Harris acknowledges the significance of silence and voice for women in the contemporary writings of women who play with these images:

> Tillie Olsen writes a series of essays entitled, "Silences"; Adrienne Rich speaks of "Lies, Secrets and Silences"; Rita Gross and Nancy Falk, writing on the religious lives of women, name them "Unspoken Worlds." Carol Gilligan calls her work "In a Different Voice"; Theodora Penny Martin entitles hers "The Sound of Our Own Voices." Exploring the emergence of women's poetry in America, Alicia Suskin Ostriker calls that experience "Stealing the Language."[10]

The power of language as metaphor is obvious. And it requires more than the attempts at "inclusive language" that have disturbed many people. Inclusive language is absolutely essential, but it alone is not enough. The power of voice, of language, must be a metaphor of women's liberation, not just a token concession, or an attempt at integration.[11] So massive is their linguistic-psychic damage that many women reach a numbed acceptance of victimization without even being aware of it. Added to this damage is the deprivation of an image of the Divine to uphold the intrinsic sanctity of being a female human. *Because* women are female, we have been deprived of our sacred rite/right of Divine Presence in an image that affirms our being and dignity. We must search for more.

The language used in this writing in reference to the Divine attempts to express both liberation and connection. When speaking of the Gods/ Goddesses or the Goddess of ancient cultures, the words are capitalized; this departs from the conventional use of lowercase, which we feel diminishes their truth and/or relevance. The God of the Judeo-Christian tradition is understood to represent a male-defined belief system and is not, by itself, adequate for this thealogy. This is not an attempt to diminish this God experience but rather to point out its androcentric nature. The Divine of this tradition is frequently referred to here as *Mother-God* to balance the divine image somewhat. The most comprehensive term used is *God/ess,* "a written symbol intended to combine both the masculine and feminine forms of the word for the divine while preserving the Judeo-Christian affirmation that divinity is one."[12] Honoring the Hebrew thought that any naming of the Divine is impossible and ought to be acknowledged as such, the word itself is unpronounceable. Furthermore, "it serves as an analytic sign to point toward that yet unnameable understanding of the divine that would transcend patriar-

chal limitations and signal redemptive experience for women as well
as men.[13]

Religion as a Symbol System

According to anthropologist Clifford Geertz,

> religion is a system of symbols which acts to establish powerful, pervasive,
> and long-lasting moods in men by formulating conceptions of a general
> order of existence and clothing these conceptions with such an aura of
> factuality that the moods and motivations seem uniquely realistic.[14]

Geertz further argues that symbols actually have the power of transforming one's worldview.[15] If symbols do possess this power—and Geertz's
arguments are persuasive—then control of the symbol system may be
equated with control of reality. Since the triumph of patriarchy approxi-
mately five thousand years ago, males have totally dominated the symbol
system and, therefore, reality.[16] This domination has led us to our present
reality, where the major question is not whether we will destroy ourselves
but only whether the means of self-destruction will be economic, nuclear,
or ecological. However, one can argue that if the symbol system were
changed, reality would also be changed. The process of coming to name
the One who creates us helps to clarify our own self-image and our
place in the cosmos. As we re-image and re-imagine our divine origins,
we allow creative responses to surface in our consciousness that naturally
spill over into our behavior. Thus the insights reflected in these pages
continue the dialogue concerning what is needed for us to change. We
also reflect the possibilities and future direction necessary for the Judeo-
Christian tradition if it is to be a viable religious system in the twenty-first
century. To bring about this change in reality, we are presenting a
symbol system that finds expression as the feminine Divine. The meanings that Western women (and men) experience through this primary
symbol of the feminine Divine are discussed in this book.[17]

The Organization of This Book

In chapter 1, "The Holy Spirit as the Feminine Divine," we theologize
on the Holy Spirit as the feminine aspect of the Divine. We begin by
examining the Hebrew tradition, in both its bibilical and its postbiblical
aspects. We then take a similar look at the Christian tradition. The
question of why the feminine Divine was lost in the Judeo-Christian
tradition and the necessity of its rediscovery are examined. We then

propose an outline of a thealogy of the Holy Spirit as the feminine Divine.

Chapter 2, "Psychological Insights into the Feminine," traces women's contemporary self-understanding of their social reality and their inner development, distinguishing the latter from the male ego experience. We comment on the insights of Jungian psychology from a feminist perspective, affirming major Jungian insights as well as noting some of its androcentric tendencies. We then explore some of the more powerful and liberating symbols and images for women related to the God/ess Within.

"The Goddess," chapter 3, reclaims the ancient, prepatriarchal Goddess tradition and explores some Goddess symbols and stories. We explain some of the possible reasons for biased interpretations of archaeological findings and sketch the destruction of matristic culture and the expropriation of women's sacred rituals and symbols. Lastly, we describe the revival of the Wicca movement today.

In chapter 4, "The Christian Trinity and the Feminine Divine," we examine the issue of androgyny and propose some contemporary androgynous models of the Christian Trinity. We explore issues that hinder the incorporation of the feminine Divine in the trinitarian context (namely, *Abba* as the name for God, and the *filioque* clause). A gender-free model of the Trinity is then proposed and the subject of duality is examined. We conclude by projecting our understanding for the future development of the models of the feminine Divine examined in chapters 1 and 4.

Chapter 5, "The Feminist Mystic/Prophet" explores the feminine Divine within the Judeo-Christian tradition as a process of personal conversion. This process, usually associated with the mystical tradition, includes the union of the mystical and the prophetic experiences within a feminist justice-oriented context. Briefly outlined are four models from the mystical tradition that can be interpreted from this perspective: our sources are the writings of Julian of Norwich, Mechtild of Magdeburg, Meister Eckhart, and Hildegard of Bingen. We conclude with a few brief personal accounts written by women today.

In chapter 6: "What Was, What Is, What Will Be," we review the time when the feminine Divine was worshiped: the matricentric age. We then review the time when She was no longer honored: the patriarchal age. An eco-feminist critique of patriarchy is then proposed. This is followed by an examination of the relationship between the political and the personal. We conclude by looking at the vision that is needed to guide us in the omnicentric age.

Eleanor Rae is primarily responsible for chapters 1, 4, and 6, while

Bernice Marie-Daly is primarily responsible for chapters 2, 3, and 5. The introduction is an equally shared labor.

Ultimately liberation is grounded in the feminine Divine as the enabling energy that stimulates our imagination to create new divine symbols and images, that allows for a religious symbol system and myth uniting cosmology and spirituality, that enpowers us to believe the not yet:

Come Holy Spirit, fill our hearts with faith in creation and enkindle in us the fire of Your love. Send forth Your Spirit so that we can be re-created and renew through You the face of the earth.

Chapter One

The Holy Spirit as the Feminine Divine

She has been there from the beginning. Her Presence was intuited by our ancestors, slowly, experience by experience. They began the gathering of the words and images that will one day come together to reveal to us her proper name. In the meantime, we can only continue to move toward completing the process begun by those who went before us—to look at the images and words that history has preserved for us concerning the feminine Divine and to add our own insights to this yet-to-be-finished mosaic. While Her images are to be found in many traditions, in this chapter, we will limit our discussion to the Judeo-Christian tradition. Specifically, we will look at the possibility the tradition presents for experiencing the feminine Divine as the Holy Spirit.

The Hebrew Scriptures

Long before it was written down, the story of the creation of women and men in the image of the Divine was told by the Hebrew peoples. In time, their story was recorded and preserved for us by the priestly writer. In Genesis 1:26–27, he speaks of the Creator who says, "Let us make humankind in our image, after our likeness," and of the human race, which, in being created in the Divine image, was created both female and male. If this is the reality of creation, we are led to conclude that "There must be in God, in a transcendent form, something that corresponds to masculinity and something that corresponds to femininity."[1] The One who creates is identified by the plural name *Elohim*, which is why creation is spoken of as being in *Our* image. Thus the dialectic of the one and the many is seen as residing with the Divinity itself. Humankind, which is in the image and likeness of God, is also one and many. The singular is *Adam,* the collective term for humankind,

9

which carries no sexual connotation. But the story goes on to say that, as well as singular, we are plural: male and female in our image and likeness of the Divine. Neither female nor male alone is the image and likeness of the Divine; only both together are this image.[2]

The Divine in its masculine aspect has been emphasized throughout the ages. But Hebrew Scripture is not devoid of references to the transcendent feminine. Scattered throughout the Old Testament are images reflecting the feminine qualities of the Divine, for example, the image of tenderness found in Hosea and Jeremiah as well as Second and Third Isaiah.[3] The word for tenderness is *rahamin* ("bowels"), which is the plural of *rehem* ("womb").[4] In addition to this more obvious feminine imagery, contemporary biblical scholars are suggesting translations that uncover previously obscured imagery of the feminine Divine. D. F. Stramara would translate *El Shaddai* (a name for the Divine in the Old Testament) as "God the breasted one." In Hebrew, the word for breast is *shad,* while *ai* is the feminine ending such as one finds in *Sarai.* Stramara proposes that the origin of this imagery is not particularly ethereal; rather, one need only look at the shape of a mountain to grasp its origin. Further, *El Shaddai* is linked to the breath or Spirit of God, as in Job 33:4: "God's breath it was that made me, the breathing of *Shaddai* that gave me life."[5]

The term for the breath or spirit of God is a feminine term: *ruah.* It occurs frequently (three hundred seventy-eight times) in the Old Testament. In about one-third of these instances *ruah* refers to the life of God, that is, the force by which God acts or causes action; it is life-energy. This spirit may be referred to as "holy" because it comes from God and in fact belongs to the heart of God's very existence.[6] This holy Breath, or Spirit, is experienced as enlightenment or as the mind of God. Eventually, this perception of the functioning of the divine Spirit as enlightenment led some of the biblical writers to perceive something of her transcendent divine reality. For the Hebrew sages, she becomes the transcendent Wisdom of God,[7] which in Hebrew is rendered by the feminine term *hokhmah.*

However, *hokhmah,* or "Wisdom," is not presented merely as a concept by the Hebrew sages. Rather, she is personified as a woman.[8] She may be characterized as God's way of being or acting, especially in reference to the world.[9] Wisdom is spoken of in terms that are usually reserved for God alone. She is everywhere, orders all things well, and can do all things. Her greatest work is to enter holy souls and make them friends of God and prophets (Wisd. 7:27–81). Wisdom is depicted as a divine saving figure, guiding Noah to safety, calling Abraham, and leading the Hebrew people and Moses through the sea to safety

(Wisd. 10:1ff.). Baruch 3 indicates that Wisdom existed in her own right before creation and that, in fact, Yahweh needed her to begin the creative process.[10] When she speaks, she speaks not as a prophet, but "by herself, on her own authority, like a goddess."[11] The teaching on Wisdom culminates in the close identification between Wisdom and the Spirit. In fact, they are so closely identified that the two may be seen as the same reality, particularly as they are viewed in their actions.[12] They may be characterized as "God for us and with us."[13]

Postbiblical Judaism

The experience of the Hebrew people that God was with them continued to be expressed by the postbiblical writers. The word used to convey this experience was *shekinah*, a feminine Aramaic term derived from the Biblical *shakan*, "to inhabit." Thus, where Exodus 25:8 would say, "Let them make me a sanctuary that I may dwell among them," the Aramaic translation (paraphrase *Targum Onkelos*) reads, "I will cause my presence ["*shekinah*"] to abide among them." *Shekinah* conveys presence experienced as light; *shekinah* is a reverential way of saying "God."[14] According to Raphael Patai, *shekinah* is the successor to the biblical Wisdom or enlightenment. *Shekinah* is the aspect of deity that can be apprehended by the senses. While initially the term *shekinah* may have been used to counteract an overly explicit anthropomorphism rather than to deal with the issue of the feminine in God, the focus in time shifted to the feminine.

It was a widely held belief that wherever the Hebrew people went in their exile, the *shekinah* accompanied them and would stay with them until their redemption. Good deeds, no matter whose they were, attracted her; when the prophets of Baal were hospitable, she descended upon them and rested there. The significance of the *shekinah* reached its peak in late Midrash literature when she came to be regarded as an independent feminine divine entity who, motivated by her compassion for people, argued against God in their defense. The Holy Spirit was also seen as coming to the defense of a sinful Israel, and Patai believes that the terms *shekinah* and *Holy Spirit* were used interchangeably during the Talmudic period.[15]

Growing out of the Talmud (and looking back even earlier, to Philo), is the Cabala, a great Jewish mystical movement that reached its zenith in the thirteenth century with the writing of the *Zohar*. At this time, the *shekinah* is explicitly developed as the feminine side of God. The deep-seated human need to experience God/ess as feminine is attested by the fact that this tenet of the cabalistic movement gained wide acceptance, reaching its height in popularity in the sixteenth and seventeenth centuries.[16] And, as would be expected, when the feminine in God is addressed, woman as being in the divine image is also addressed. Thus, the *Zohar* reads:

> This is the book of the generations of Adam. On the day that God created Adam, in the likeness of God He created him; male and female He created them. He blessed them and called their name Adam on the day they were created. (Gen. 5:1–2)
> Rabbi Shim said
> High mysteries are revealed in these two verses. Male and Female He [*sic*] created them to make known the glory on high, the mystery of faith. Out of this mystery, Adam was created.
> Male and female he [*sic*] created them. From here we learn:
> Any image that does not embrace male and female is not a high and true image.
> We have established this in the mystery of our Midrash.
> Come and see:
> The Blessed Holy One does not place His abode in any place where male and female are not found together. Blessings are found only in a place where male and female are found, as it is written:
> "He blessed them and called their name Adam on the day they were created."
> It is not written: "He blessed him and called his name Adam." A human being is only called Adam when male and female are one.[17]

While the above gives a flavor of the *shekinah,* or the presence of the feminine Divine among us, it would be well to note that this experience of God/ess came from a long and venerable history. It is the heir of the biblical "cloud of glory" that had dwelt in the sanctuary as the visible manifestation of Yahweh's presence. When the Temple was destroyed and Yahweh withdrew to heaven, the *shekinah* remained on earth, directly accessible to her people. Her descent upon humankind and her dwelling among the people is considered a rupture in the Divine Self. Even today, the *shekinah* shares the suffering of people and, in fact, is the one who suffers most. But in the end, God and the *shekinah* will be united.[18] In the meantime, she is the only God we know. In other words, our only knowledge of God is through her.[19] Expounding on the rabbinical doctrine of the immanence of God, Joshua Abelson sees this doctrine as expressed primarily as *shekinah* and/or Holy Spirit. While he would not see them as identical, he regards these two terms as bearing a strong affinity for one another.[20] Yves Congar also notes that the Old Testament authors speak of the *shekinah* in a way similar to the way in which New Testament authors speak of the Holy Spirit when they refer to God's indwelling activity.[21]

The New Testament and the Noncanonical Writings

The theme of the indwelling of the Holy Spirit is especially prominent in Paul and John.[22] In addition, Luke employs the term "full of the Spirit," initially in reference to Jesus and later when referring to the disciples.[23] In his paper "The Holy Spirit as Woman in Apocalypse 12," Gilles Quispel sees the woman in the Apocalypse as being the Holy Spirit accompanying the Christian community in its flight into exile just as the *shekinah* accompanied the people of Yahweh into exile.[24] Along with the themes of indwelling and presence, the feminine attribute of tenderness is employed by the New Testament writers. In the Old Testament Yahweh was shown to have the love and the disposition of a mother, and the Gospels depict Jesus, the one who was full of the Spirit, in the same terms.[25]

The Old Testament image of Wisdom as a feminine aspect of the Divine is picked up by Jesus and his disciples. Luke quotes Jesus as saying, "Yet, wisdom is justified by all her children" (Luke 7:35). In the verses preceding this remark, Jesus talks about his own rejection, as well as that of John the Baptist. Neither was able to save all of the people. Yet each, with their contrasting life-styles, was able to bring salvation to some. Jesus would seem to suggest that it is only Wisdom who is able to be the universal saving presence. Thus she is seen as justified by John and Jesus and possibly by others. Moreover, in Paul (1 Cor. 2:4–16) one finds the correlation of wisdom and the Spirit, calling to mind the identification of wisdom and the Spirit found in Wisdom 7:22.[26] However, it should be noted here that while the image of the Holy Spirit as the feminine Divine develops naturally from the Hebrew use of the feminine word *ruah* ("spirit"), subsequent translations of Scripture did not support this development. Thus the Greek of the New Testament rendered the Spirit as *pneuma*, which is neuter, while the Latin used the word *spiritus,* which is masculine. Nonetheless, strands of the development of the Holy Spirit as the feminine in God are to be found in the Christian tradition. But before turning to this development, let us look briefly at the Gnostic writings to see what they reveal concerning the feminine imaging of God/ess.

The writers of the Gnostic gospels often viewed God not only as the Divine Father, but also as the Divine Mother. According to Elaine Pagels, these writings may be grouped in three different categories. In the first category, the Divine is seen as a dyad of the Divine Mother and the Divine Father. The Divine Mother in this dyad is variously imaged as Grace, Silence, the Womb, the Mother of All, and Intelligence (in Greek, the feminine term *epinoia*). She is the source of all that is, including, in some accounts, even the great God Yahweh Himself. A second group of writings describes the Divine Mother as the Holy Spirit. Thus, for example, in the Apocryphone of John, she is seen as Mother in a trinitarian vision; in the Gospel of Thomas, Jesus contrasts his earthly parents, Mary and Joseph, to his Divine Mother, the Holy Spirit, and to his Divine Father; in the Gospel of Philip, the Spirit is called the "Mother of many."[27] The Gospel to the Hebrews, which is utilized by Clement of Alexandria, Origen, and Jerome, also speaks of the Holy Spirit as Mother. For example, Origen quotes, "Even so did my mother, the Holy Spirit, take me by one of my hairs and carry me away on to the great mountain Tabor," while Jerome sees the Holy Spirit as Mother descending on Jesus at his baptism.[28] Finally, there are some Gnostic writers who characterized the Divine Mother as Wisdom. As such she is called the source of all creation, the one who enlightens humanity and makes it wise, the savior of Noah and his family from the wrath of God the Father, the coincidence of opposites, the first and the last.[29]

Elaine Pagels, who is interested both in biblical scholarship and in cultural issues, asks the question, Did the Gnostic Christian women derive any practical social advantages from this feminine conceptualization of the Divine? Her answer is yes, as evidenced by the fact that women were revered as prophets, teachers, exorcists, and healers; that they presided at eucharist and baptism; that they were ordained as priests and bishops; that they were founders of Gnostic movements. While she does not always see a universal connection, she does conclude that the weight of the evidence indicates a clear correlation between Gnostic religious theory and social practice.[30] This issue of correlation between religious theory and social practice will be looked at in orthodox Christianity when we examine "the loss of the tradition," but we first need to look at the development of the experience of the Holy Spirit as the feminine Divine within the mainstream of Christianity.

The Christian Tradition

Within mainstream Christianity, as in the Gnostic writings, the Holy Spirit was experienced in explicitly sexual terms. She is called Mother, Spouse, the New Eve, Sister, Daughter. Traces of these experiences are found in mystical, liturgical, and theological writings. In Ebionism, a tradition that may be characterized as Judeo-Christian in origin, we find the vision of Elkesai. In this vision, he sees two beings of equal and immense dimensions. The masculine he identifies as the Son of God, while the feminine he sees as the Holy Spirit.[31]

Within the Syriac liturgical tradition, a tradition that was also Judeo-Christian, we find the Holy Spirit imaged as the feminine in God/ess. The signing in the rite of initiation, the laying on of hands in the rite of ordination, and the eucharistic sacrifice were effected by the power of the Holy Spirit, whose action is described as hovering or brooding.[32] She is imaged in the context of the liturgy as a merciful mother.[33] This understanding of the Holy Spirit as feminine Divine was evident in the Syriac liturgy until A.D. 400.[34]

In theological writings the Holy Spirit also is represented in sexual images. In *Against Heresies* (3. 24:1) Irenaeus states, "Those who do not have a share in the Spirit are not nourished to life by the Mother's breasts." Likewise, Clement of Alexandria characterizes God in feminine as well as in masculine terms. He refers to the Word as mother, nurse, and teacher, while the Father nourishes us with milk from His breasts. On this basis, in what seems to be a pattern, Clement sees men and women as sharing equally in perfection, and urges women to participate with men in the community. He backs up his urging for female participation by listing women who have held prominent places in history as rulers, writers, philosophers, poets, and painters.[35] While Clement imaged both the Father and the Word in feminine terms, Methodius of Olympus (d. 311) looked specifically to the Holy Spirit and saw Her as Bride and as the New Eve.[36] For Synesius of Cyrene (d. after 412), the Holy Spirit was Mother, Sister, and Daughter. Congar makes the point that this is not the thinking of the Gnostics only; rather, he would see it as being an early part of the common Christian tradition.[37] For the orthodox Syriac theologians, it was commonplace to refer to the Holy Spirit as She. According to R. Murray, these Syriac theologians are "simply attributing to the Holy Spirit the motherly character which the latter parts of Isaiah (49:14–15; 66:13) find in God."[38]

As well as the images of the Holy Spirit as mother, spouse, the new Eve, sister, and daughter, She appears to us in our tradition as divine Wisdom. Some of the early church fathers, for example, Theophilus of Antioch, Irenaeus, and the author of the Clementine Homilies, regarded Wisdom in the Old Testament as prefiguring the Holy Spirit.[39] Justin Martyr also equated the divine intelligence with the Holy Spirit; however, he diverged from biblical pneumatology in that he also equated the divine intelligence with the Logos, or Son. For Clement of Alexandria, there was only one principle of enlightenment, the Son. While this imaging of Wisdom as the Son rather than as the Holy Spirit is the basic path followed by Origen, Augustine, and Aquinas, there is an alternate path that does follow the biblical witness. Thus, for Irenaeus, the Father is unknown, transcendent, and mysterious; the Son is the one who executes the Father's will; the Spirit is the divine Wisdom who nourishes, increases, and illumines. This way of theologizing is developed by Gaius Marius Victorinus (baptized circa 354). For Victorinus, the Son is the action of the Father, the one through whom the Divine Being is channeled outward and downward into matter; the Spirit is the Divine Intelligence, the living thought of God that leads us back to the Divinity.[40]

While this understanding of Wisdom (*sophia*) as the feminine aspect of the Divine remained basically undeveloped in the Christian tradition (for reasons which we will examine in the next section), there are attempts in relatively recent times to develop a sophiology. In the Russian Orthodox tradition, Vladimir Soloviev (1853–1900) drew on three religious experiences he had with *sophia*, whom he acknowledges as the model of feminine beauty. For Soloviev, She was the first expression of God and the Mother of all of Creation. Further, She was the soul of the world, as well as the divine purpose and vision in view of which the universe is made. However, as well as drawing on Christian sources, he turned to non-Christian sources such as the cabala, which led to his being held suspect and his sophiology remaining undeveloped.[41] Soloviev was not the first theologian to have such an experience of censure when attempting to develop a theology of the feminine aspect of the Divine.

The Loss of the Tradition

The preceding discussion indicates that there is a good basis in the Judeo-Christian tradition for the development of an understanding of the Holy Spirit as the feminine aspect of the Divine. We realize, however, that this development has not yet occurred. We will now look at our history to see why such an understanding of the Holy Spirit has remained undeveloped in our tradition.

In Scripture the most obvious avenue for the development of the Holy Spirit as the feminine aspect of the Deity is provided by the Old Testament concept of Wisdom. As we have seen, both Wisdom and Spirit are designated by feminine words in Hebrew Scriptures and are very closely linked; some even see them as identical. But rather than developing the Holy Spirit as the feminine divine Wisdom, the New Testament writers basically transferred the attributes of Wisdom to

Christ. This happened both directly and indirectly. In Paul, for example, there is a direct identification and substitution of Christ for Wisdom (1 Cor. 1:24, 30). Thus Paul says that Christ is with God at the beginning (cf. Prov. 8:22–31); is sent to Israel (cf. Sir. 24:11–34); is savior (cf. Wisd. 10); protects and preserves the godly (cf. Prov. 4:6); is the law (cf. Sir. 24:24); is life itself (cf. Prov. 8:35). In John, by contrast, Wisdom is superseded by the Logos, which is then identified with Christ. John identifies Christ with the feminine in three ways: by means of the Prologue, where the activities and attributes of Wisdom are predicated of the Word; by putting the "I am" statements of Wisdom (who in the Old Testament speaks for herself) into the mouth of Jesus; and by portraying Jesus as the one who is nurturing and caring. In both Paul and John, the result is the same: a feminine hypostasis of God is transformed into a masculine one.[42] (This same type of transformation is still apparent in our own day. In the commentary on the reading of Prov. 8:22–31 for Trinity Sunday, we are told: "The praise of Wisdom is a kind of foreshadowing of the doctrine of the Blessed Trinity. Wisdom is personified as the creative spirit of God speaking in her [sic] own person and later to be manifested in the person of Jesus Christ.")[43]

While the transference of the attributes of the feminine Wisdom primarily to Christ rather than to the Holy Spirit occurred in the New Testament, we nevertheless saw that the tradition began to develop an understanding of the Holy Spirit as the feminine aspect of the Divine. This development was quite truncated, however, primarily because the Spirit as feminine came to be increasingly identified with Gnostic circles and because the human need to find the feminine in the Divine was satisfied by the development of feminine images of the church and of Mary.[44] But before looking at these alternative developments of the feminine in ecclesiology and Mariology, let us look more deeply at the development of the relationship between Wisdom and the Word that was established by the New Testament authors.

Christology was influenced not only by the writers Paul and John and their understanding of the relationship between Wisdom and the Word. Philo, a Jewish philosopher who lived during the changing of the millennium, also dealt with this relationship—Wisdom, mediated through his Jewish background and the Word, mediated through his Hellenistic culture. He developed the concepts of Wisdom and the Word as distinct but equal: for example, Wisdom is God's Daughter while the Word is God's Son. In Philo, however, the Word eventually takes over Wisdom's functions. So it is the Word rather than Wisdom who represents divine order, the law, the teacher, the firstborn of creation, the nurturer of humans, that is, the one who lives among the people. Wisdom is relegated to heaven, where she is still regarded as Mother of the World, its beginning and its end.

Philo's influence on early Christian theologians is at least threefold. First, he removed Wisdom from the world and restricted her to heaven, where she is described as the ever-virgin Daughter of God (language that is later picked up in the writings about Mary). Second, he propagated a negative attitude toward the feminine: for Philo, the male was normative while the female was material, corruptible, and something to be overcome. Third, he changed the sex of the active, powerful Wisdom into that of the male Logos; thus the male Logos fills the roles and functions that formerly were attributed to the feminine Wisdom.[45]

The early church fathers—for example, the Shepherd of Hermes, Justin Martyr, Clement, and Origen—continued to develop Christology along the lines of Paul and John (and Philo) in that they attributed to Jesus the qualities and function of Wisdom. But this led to problems in that Jewish monotheism insisted on the subordinate status of Wisdom in relationship to Yahweh. Analogously, this line of theologizing seemed to call for a subordinate status for Jesus in regard to God: Jesus is not seen as equal to the Father, but rather as the firstborn of all creation. This understanding of Jesus reached its height in the Arian heresy, a controversy that was resolved by declaring the Son equal to the Father. This declaration of the Word's equality with the Father was accomplished at the expense of the Wisdom tradition, a tradition that seemed to stand in the way of Jesus' divinity.[46] (Nonetheless, through the ages, feminine qualities and attitudes—such as the feeding with milk, gentleness, and love—have been celebrated in Christ, giving rise to the devotion to Christ as our Mother. This may be seen, for example, in the ideals set by the great abbots and Cistercian monks of the twelfth century, as well as in the writings of Julian of Norwich, a fifteenth-century mystic.)[47]

But the powerful symbol of Mother is seen primarily not in the person of Jesus, but rather in the image of the church and in the person of Mary. Moreover, ecclesiology was developed through the use of the feminine images of Wisdom and Bride. By taking on the attributes of Wisdom—for example, as a teacher who trains, punishes, and chastises—"she" (the church) was able to attribute enormous powers to "herself," namely, the powers of the magisterium.[48] However, because it is so obviously a human institution, the church ultimately must fail as a symbol of the feminine Divine.

The imaging of Mary as a symbol of the feminine divine is more complex. Joan Chamberlain Engelsman finds attributed to Mary five qualities that are otherwise found only in the goddesses of the Hellenistic world. These are her miraculous conception, her perpetual virginity, her bodily assumption into heaven, her status as "Mother of God," and her status as co-redemptrix.[49] The attribution to Mary of these qualities may be regarded as not altogether fortuitous. On the one hand, they make her a quasi goddess in spite of the insistence that she is absolutely human. On the other hand, they make it virtually impossible for us to identify with her.

However, Mary was also eventually identified with Wisdom. We have already noted how the equation of Wisdom with the Logos fell into disfavor because of the Arian controversy. But the texts that made it apparent that Wisdom was, in fact, a person, were eventually applied to Mary. Beginning in the seventh century, Sirach 24 was applied to virgins and martyrs: the wise were those who had with certainty attained union with God. Over time, this text came to be applied to Mary, the virgin par excellence. By contrast, Proverbs 8 was applied to Mary without the necessity of a middle step. This application is evident in a liturgy from the tenth century that was developed for the celebration of Mary's nativity.[50] However, while Mary as a symbol for the femininity of God may work for some in that she reveals to us a Divinity who possesses feminine qualities,[51] she ultimately fails as this symbol because, despite all the accolades, she is, alas, like us, merely a creature. In summary, it may be said that the repression of the feminine Divine was extremely successful. Since Jesus is male, direct access to the feminine Divine is not possible. And the church and Mary fail as images because, in reality, they are merely human.[52]

We have traced briefly the history of the suppression of the feminine Divine. Can we go beneath these events to detect the attitudinal climate that helps to explain them? Pagels points out to us the correlation between religious theory and social practice. She sees a connection between imaging the Divine as feminine and a resulting social equality of women. While admitting that this connection is not universal, she presents enough evidence to enable this connection to be seen as a pattern. For example, she argues for a correlation between the "orthodox" masculine God and the eventual suppression of women's early roles. She sees cultural elements winning out against Jesus' own attitude, which was one of openness to women despite the culture of his time.[53] In contrast to Pagels, Engelsman sees the repression of the feminine dimension of the Divine to be based on what she calls "Philo's law of preeminence," according to which "preeminence always pertains to the masculine, and the feminine always comes short of and is lesser than it."[54] In other words, anything feminine cannot be divine and anything divine must be masculine. This "law" was applied by relegating the feminine Divine to the status of creature (for example, Mary or the church) or by changing the sex of the feminine Divine, as when Wisdom was turned into the Logos, or Christ.[55]

The Necessity of Rediscovering the Feminine Divine

It is not only Pagels who sees the connection between the repression of the feminine aspect of the Deity and the repression of women. Yves Congar also thinks that a neglect of the Holy Spirit has led, in society in general but especially in the church, to patriarchy and an overemphasis on the masculine. Consequently, he sees the church as

> now confronted with a twofold task—on the one hand, it has to become more fully both masculine and feminine and, on the other, it has to preserve feminine values without keeping women in the "harem" of passive and charming qualities from which they wish to emerge to be treated simply and authentically as persons.[56]

While Congar concentrates on the church as the area which is most in need of imaging the feminine aspect of the Divine, J. Edgar Bruns finds this need particularly in the world. He sees the female image as generally identified with the exercise of intelligence and the creation of civilization. His writing further suggests that "there is a deep need, sensed in all periods, to endow the divine with a feminine aspect—which, if neglected or denied, can find expression in destructive ways."[57] The more obvious of those destructive ways in our own time can be seen in our ecological crisis[58] and in our nuclear crisis. A question must be asked: Would we continue to rape the earth, and plan for her ultimate destruction, if we truly saw the earth as the place where the Holy Spirit is embodied, if we recognized that there is no atom in the universe where she is not present? If, as Ira Chenus suggests,[59] the issues must be solved on the mythological rather than on the rational level, then the question of who God/ess is, is the ultimate practical question. However, before addressing this question of a contemporary theology of the Holy Spirit as the feminine Divine, it would be well to look at two areas where this issue of how we image God/ess is critical: the area of worship and that of language.

We humans have worshiped the Other since the dawn of our understanding. History's first recorded poem is a hymn to the goddess Inanna by the priestess Enheduanna.[60] And we continue to experience this need to worship—a need that exists not on the part of the Divine but on our part. It has been suggested that "we become what we worship, since we worship what we value ultimately and absolutely."[61] If who we are—and ultimately what the world is to become—is determined by the images we choose in our worship, then we must self-consciously look at and evaluate the images we have chosen, to determine whether they in fact represent that which is truly valuable and deserving of worship. We must ask ourselves what is the appropriate response when we find our present images inadequate because, for example, they embody only masculine values without the feminine values for which today's crises so radically call. It may be that, in order to answer this radical call, the image of Wisdom (*Sophia*), for example, can be adequately developed within the patriarchal structure.[62] Or it may be necessary to form feminist liturgical exodus communities that would exist for a transitional period until feminine values and images become part of the existing system.[63] Or it may be that the only hope lies in the establishment of a feminist post-Christian liturgy and world view.[64] The choice of the appropriate avenue is not apparent at this time; what should be apparent is the necessity of choosing an avenue that will lead to shrines where She may be worshiped and Her values taken up in order to bring about the transformation of ourselves and of our world.

Just as the issue of who we worship and who we become is one of reciprocity, so also is the issue of language and reality. While it may be perceived that language shapes our sense of reality, it may also be perceived that reality shapes our sense of language. This double reference may also be seen in regard to symbols: a symbol serves as a model of a community's sense of ultimate reality and as a model for human behavior and social order. A concrete example of this modeling may be seen in reference to God/ess and the Sabbath. God/ess is the one who rests on the seventh day. If this is so, then are we not also called to rest on the seventh day and, in doing so, do we not become more like God/ess? This analysis may be applied to male God language: the language both tells us who God is (male) and justifies a community that gives power and authority to men.[65] Some would argue that the traditional images of Deity (for example, God the Father) are nonsexual symbols.[66] However, it is not possible to have a personal God who is gender-free. To be a person implies sex—male or female; we have no other models.[67] "The metaphor of a gender-free person is impossible."[68] "Equally, no set of religious images has ever spoken of a personal Ultimate without the use of masculine and/or feminine imagery as a tool."[69] Making peace with anthropomorphism is the price we pay for having a personal God/ess rather than a nonpersonal Ultimate.[70] Rather than God as Father being exalted above all sexuality,

He has in fact been exalted above female sexuality only. This results in the destruction of the personhood of those who do not mirror the male imaging of Divine personhood.[71] Also, we might ask ourselves, if we do not in fact mean that God is male when we use masculine imagery and pronouns, then why are objections raised to the use of female imagery and pronouns?[72] To summarize, it may be said that, by definition, the Judeo-Christian Ultimate is sexual; that is what being a person means.

The Holy Spirit and the Trinity

If the rediscovery of the feminine Divine is necessary for our own and our world's survival, the most obvious place to find Her would be in the person of the Holy Spirit. This is simply because this is where the feminine in God/ess has already been experienced in Judeo-Christian Scripture and tradition. I would further propose that we look at the Holy Spirit as the feminine in God/ess within the trinitarian context. I do this for a simple reason: I desire to remain within the tradition. However, when we look at the Holy Spirit within the context of the Trinity, we are immediately confronted with a difficulty: the issue of unbalance. In the teaching on the Trinity, the First Person (Father) and the Second Person (Son) have usually been presented as male. So it would seem that even if the Holy Spirit is imaged and worshiped as the feminine in God/ess, we are still living with a Divinity who is more masculine than feminine, with the resulting implication that, in the human creation, the male is more godly. However, if we accept the basic equality of female and male in creation, and work out of the mode of theologizing that compares the form to the Former, we would be led to posit a balance of masculinity and femininity within the trinitarian life itself. Our next step would then be to suggest models within the tradition which present such a balance.

Sergius Bulgakov (1870–1944), when theologizing on the mystery of the Trinity, finds at its heart the One who cannot be known unless the choice is made for self-revelation. But, in fact, the Divinity does reveal itself—as ultimate Wisdom. This eternal Wisdom is manifested in two hypostases—that of the Son and that of the Spirit. This is how Divinity reveals itself to itself. The Deity is also revealed to the outside world through the process of creation. Corresponding to the divine Wisdom, there is the created Wisdom, the image of God, manifested through the cosmos and especially through humankind. For Bulgakov, the Father is both eternal abyss and eternal light.[73] Sophia (Wisdom) is the Mother, the Womb where the creaturely Wisdom is conceived.

The divine Sophia cannot be adequately revealed as the masculine Word or as the feminine Spirit but only as both. So also humanity is not adequately manifested as man or woman, but only as both. In other words, the polarity of the sexes belongs intrinsically to the structure of God.[74]

Donald L. Gelpi has also theologized on the Holy Spirit as the divine Mother within the mystery of the Trinity. Gelpi begins by searching the Scriptures for personal images of the Holy Spirit and finds that there is only one: her personification as the feminine Wisdom in the Old Testament. While he finds that few fathers of the church developed this personal imagery of the Holy Spirit—imputing instead the concept of Wisdom and her attributes to the Word—he finds exceptions in Irenaeus, Basil, and especially Victorinus. Gelpi then goes on to refute those who would object to his thesis by saying that the New Testament writers, given the opportunity, preferred masculine to feminine images of the Holy Spirit. Gelpi shows that, in fact, the images used for the Holy Spirit in the New Testament are mostly impersonal rather than either masculine or feminine.[75] He also deals with objections against using feminine archetypal images for the Holy Spirit, objections which he believes are grounded in "unconscious attitudes nurtured by the sexist, patriarchal caste of the culture in which we live."[76] Rather than reject feminine archetypal images, Gelpi suggests that we transvaluate the archetype of the feminine so that it is viewed soley as a positive, life-giving, transforming presence. As such, it provides appropriate imagery for the Holy Spirit as the feminine aspect of the Divine. Finally, Gelpi would see the need to transvaluate the archetype of the masculine in regard to Christ in order to repudiate its "macho" connotations. He would argue for regarding Christ as androgynous rather than as masculine.[77]

One further model for looking at the Holy Spirit as the feminine aspect of God/ess may be developed if we broaden our understanding of the First Person of the Trinity from simply Father to that of Parent or of Father and Mother. Scripture provides us with the images that would call for such representation.[78] And Jesus' use of the term *Abba* may not be the stumbling block that it appears to be at first glance. It has been suggested that, at its root, the term that we translate as "Father" or "Daddy" would be better rendered as "parent" in that it can be either masculine or feminine. It may also be argued that the term *Abba* speaks to the fact that Jesus knew and did God's work. But this sense of the term was lost and it came to be associated primarily with a male progenitor.[79] The original sense of the term *Abba* frees us to look at the source of the Trinity not as male ("Father") but as the Transcendent—the One who is, for example, as Bulgakov states, both eternal light and eternal abyss. The Transcendent One reveals Him/ Herself not only as Wisdom but also as Goodness, Truth, Beauty, and so forth. This revelation of Self is imparted eternally to the feminine Spirit and to the masculine Word. Together, Spirit and Word are experienced by us as the presence of the Divinity. Together, they reveal to us all the knowledge that one can have of God/ess. Together, they invite us to join in the drama of creation, a dance that we see them beginning when She moves over the waters of chaos and He speaks the words of differentiation for creation (Gen. 1:2ff.).

The Christ/Spirit Relationship

We have looked at the interdependent relationship of the Word and the Spirit within the life of the Divinity. In like fashion, one may look at the Holy Spirit and Christ as participating in a relationship that is interdependent. In addition, the Christ/Spirit relationship may be looked at in two other ways. We can look at Christ from the viewpoint of the Holy Spirit[80] or we can look at the Holy Spirit from a Christological perspective.[81] Historically, the third model mentioned—theologizing on the Holy Spirit through the perspective of Christ—has been the model used almost exclusively.[82] For this reason, we have not come to know the Holy Spirit in Her own Person, nor are we a people who may be characterized as living lives in which we are led by the Spirit. To assist us in regaining this experience of leading Holy Spirit–filled lives—an experience which was enjoyed by the early Christian community—we will look at some possibilities for theologizing on the Spirit while remaining sensitive to both of the other perspectives.

This method of looking at the Word and the Spirit so that the distinctiveness of each, as well as their unity, is honored, is not new to the Judeo-Christian tradition. We see it, for example, in Isaiah 40:6–8, where the Spirit is the *ruah* of judgment by which God/ess destroys, while the Word is the promise by which God/ess restores.[83] Or in Psalm 33:6, which states: "By the word of the Lord the heavens were made; by the breath of his [*sic*] mouth all their host." Here Word and Spirit are both associated equally in the one act of creating the cosmos.[84] George T. Montague further suggests that "only the prophets seemed to have had the perfect integration of spirit and word," that is, only they were totally committed to the words of the covenant and this because they were people of "spirit."[85] Another imaging of this model is seen in the vision of Elkesai in which he sees two beings of equal and immense dimensions; the feminine, he identifies as the Holy Spirit and the masculine as the Son of God.[86] In addition to seeing Wisdom and the Word as the two hands of the Divinity, Irenaeus employed the image of drinking from God's breasts, the drink being both the Word and the Spirit.[87] To summarize, it might be said that what is seen in the tradition is "a consistent pattern in God's actions: namely, the proceeding by means of pairs or doublets." There is in this pattern "something very profound, a kind of rule of the divine Poeticus." "God is communion in unity, unity in plurality."[88]

There are additional concepts that can be employed to assist in bringing understanding to the Christ/Spirit relationship. One such concept develops the relationship in a way that had traditionally characterized the masculine/feminine relationship, namely, through the thinking/feeling relationship. Since a prophet or prophetess may be characterized as the one who is "filled to the point of bursting with God's own feelings and emotions,"[89] it would seem that the prophetic experience should offer us deep insights into the feeling side of God/ess. The prophets/prophetesses are not necessarily interested in keeping their facts straight and their arguments "cool"; rather, they are interested in presenting the truth as God/ess experiences it. Thus, while one act of injustice may be insignificant to you and me, for the prophet/prophetess, it can spell the doom of an entire people. One unjust situation can cause the prophet/prophetess to feel that the universe itself is off center because this is how God/ess experiences injustice. The relationship of the Spirit to prophecy is expressed consistently in the Old Testament, in the stories of, for example, Balaam, Saul, Hosea, Micah, Ezekiel, and Second and Third Isaiah.[90] Also, the Spirit in Revelation 22:17 is the Spirit of prophecy who is seen throughout the New Testament writings.[91] The pouring out of the Spirit at Pentecost (Acts 2:14–39) means, in fact, that all of humankind shall prophecy. And in the Nicene Creed, the Holy Spirit is identified as speaking through prophecy. However, for all its positiveness and power, the identification of the feminine Holy Spirit with the feeling aspect of God/ess also carries with it much ambiguity. This is because for too long women have been overly identified with feelings to the neglect of their thinking powers. Also, it may be that there is legitimacy in seeing the prophetic experience as masculine. As Montague says:

> The prophetic word through which God's will for men had been revealed, has a definite "masculine" ring to it: it is command, clearly enunciated with threat or promise, or both, and it comes most often as fire, or hammer shattering rock (Jer. 23:29) or as a sword (Isa. 49:2; Heb. 4:12), or as the roar of a lion (Amos 3:8). The earth trembles at the prophetic

word as a house trembles at the footsteps of an angry father. Wisdom, on the other hand, comes as invitation, as to a banquet promising delight (9:1–6). She does not preach as if proclaiming a take-it-or-leave-it message, but *teaches* suggesting a more "incarnational" approach. Showing how God's way concords with all that is humanly good and beautiful, she speaks to the heart. Hers is not the way of command but the way of holy seduction. Her words have not only clear intelligibility but sweetness and attraction, and—let us note it here for future reference—this is because she pours out her *spirit*.

Is it too much to say that Israel is discovering that in her experience of God she needs a mother as much as a father, a teacher's chair as much as a preacher's pulpit? We can at least say that she found that if secular wisdom needed to be redeemed by prophecy, prophecy in turn needed to be tamed by wisdom.[92]

Looking at the feminine concepts of Wisdom and Mother and Spirit in this passage from Montague brings us to the possibility of developing the Christ/Spirit relationship in terms of the Word/Wisdom metaphor. As previously mentioned, this model is initially suggested in the Old Testament. There we see Wisdom and the Word as co-creators of the cosmos (Ps. 33:6), as well as co-agents in the drama of re-creation (Isa. 40:6–8). For Irenaeus, only one is called God, while the Word and the Spirit function as the two hands of God.[93] As mirror images of one another, Wisdom is the one who fathoms the depth of the mind of God/ess because Wisdom is, in Herself, divine intelligence; the Word is the one who speaks and acts in total obedience to the will of God/ess, the Transcendent One—doing this historically in the person of Jesus. Together, and only together, Wisdom and Word—Holy Spirit and Christ—can bring us into the beauty and majesty of the Transcendent One.

The Spirit as the Feminine Divine

Having focused on the Holy Spirit in Her "other worldly" relationships—within the Trinity and in regard to the Christ—it is now time to look at Her as She is present to us in this world. We must ask ourselves where we would expect to find Her. The most obvious place to look would be in relationship to the church.[94] While all "believers" would probably be in agreement in seeing the Holy Spirit as intimately related to the church, the disagreements would arise over exactly how this relationship is to be expressed.[95] Edward O'Connor tells us that, because of the *pneumatomachoi*, the first theological speculation on the Spirit was directed toward Her person and not Her works—that, in fact, the question of the function of the Spirit still remains a matter in need of adequate theological formulation.[96] An added dimension in the Christian understanding of the functioning of the Holy Spirit in the church was given by Luther, and to an extent by Calvin, when, to the theological principles of authority and reason, they added the principle of religious experience. This principle, which was considered a testimony of the Holy Spirit, in time assumed the place of primacy in relation to authority and reason.[97] This question of the priority which should be placed on authority and reason on the one hand, and on religious experience on the other, and the relationship of both to the Holy Spirit, still remains unsettled today.[98]

A further dimension of the unresolved issues of the relationship between authority and religious experience, and their relationship to the Holy Spirit, arises when we consider the radical freedom of the Holy Spirit. As Albert C. Outler observes,

> Orthodoxy has tended to subordinate pneumatology to the doctrine of the church—since the notion of the radical freedom of the Spirit tends to dissolve fixed patterns of church order and ecclesiastical discipline.[99]

This question of the radical freedom of the Spirit has vast implications for the whole life of the church. To all those within the structure, She, who is Herself radical freedom, offers the opportunity to join Her as co-creators. But one cannot join her unless one is open to discerning Her path—a path that may be radically different from any we can imagine.

However, Her presence in the world is not limited to church structures.[100] Rather, it may be said that there is no corner of the universe in which She is not present; there is no speck of dust, no grain of sand, where She is not. For if She is not there—whether in a distant galaxy or in the mud on our shoes—nothing could exist. She is, as it were, incarnated—embodied—in the universe. This being so, our role in relationship to Her may be seen as that of caretakers of the body of God/ess. And who better to act as caretakers than those who are created in Her image?

While all human beings are created in the image of God/ess, it would seem that She is especially present to those people who perform the work of creation together with Her. To enjoy Her presence in a special way, it is not necessary for a person to acknowledge Her as present; it is only necessary that one be engaged in the work of the Holy Spirit.[101] But by what criteria can one discern whether the work performed is truly that of the Spirit? I would suggest that the Holy Spirit may be judged to be present in those situations where love is manifested. Thus, the Christian is called to deeper relationship and dialogue with all persons of goodwill, including those of the non-Christian religions and in atheistic ideologies. Conversely, if love is the criterion of the Spirit's presence, then Christians must ask themselves the meaning of church situations that are characterized by an absence of love.

In every age, the Spirit, who is Embodied Love, calls a people to act with Her on those issues that are most critical. In our own time, the Holy Spirit seems to be centering Her presence and activity in areas where unjust structures are being challenged and, ultimately, transformed; in the care of the earth—and, indeed, of the cosmos, because She is incarnated within it; and in the giving of love, especially to the enemy, whether that enemy be personal or political. As we move more completely into these areas, we will rediscover Her as those who have gone before us have found Her: as Wisdom; as the Mind of God/ess; as Relationship; as Love; as the feeling aspect of God/ess; as Creator; as Ruler; as Mother, Daughter, Sister, the New Eve; as the Presence of God/ess; as Radical Freedom; as the Embodiment of God/ess in the Universe. And in names yet to be revealed. As the Eternal Feminine, She invites each of us—woman and man—to use these images and thereby learn about Her. It is an invitation; She will not force Herself upon anyone. But She guarantees that the riches to be found through the acceptance of Her offer surpass what you and I can imagine.

Chapter Two

Psychological Insights into the Feminine

Scientists discover and theologians affirm; but faced with the mystery of life and death we know almost nothing. We can learn from the experts, but our experience may not fit their theories and it is our experience and our experience alone that we should trust.

—Irene Claremont de Castillejo

A common theme expressed in women's writings today is the significance of personal experience. Women are learning to trust and value their own knowing. Inasmuch as spiritual growth proceeds in conjunction with personal growth, women's contemporary self-articulation brings us to a new understanding of the female psyche in relation to that which we have called the spiritual.

In this chapter, I intend to present the contributions of contemporary women's self-understanding through a description of women's social reality. Then I will explore some aspects of Jungian psychology, with an eye on some of the aids and stumbling blocks this perspective holds, for women in particular. With these two sections as a backdrop, I will then focus on some of the images and symbols that can help women appreciate the recovery of our own sacred image depicted as aspects of the feminine Divine.

The personal journey, intertwined with the spiritual, is radically different for women from what it is for men. Women's journey must be experienced and expressed in explicitly female terms. We are struggling for a deepening self-understanding in a patriarchal culture, reflected in part by a misogynist psychology. We must return to our own story, our own experience, to know the meaning of our own inner wisdom. Modifications of some Jungian concepts, such as Self, ego development, animus, and the journey itself, can be helpful. However, our search for the Divine Within must be stripped as much as possible from patriar-

chal identifications, consciously as well as in our beginning understand-
ings of the unconscious.

In our spiritual search, we must articulate a fully embodied female
Goddess, approachable in Western Christian civilization only through
the symbol of the Virgin Mary. For women, Goddess is fully inclusive
of dark and light representing the ebb and flow of life, of transforming energy. While Mary represents for us some of the godly qualities
we are searching for, her image has been so deformed by androcentric religious bias that many people suspect it is beyond repair.
We are seeking a depth experience of what a sacred image would
mean for us.

In this approach to women's experience, I intend to weave together
the ideas of several disciplines. My assertion is threefold. First, women's
social reality has shaped women's ego development and journey story
so that it is significantly different from that assumed by male norms.
Second, Jungian psychology is problematic for some women: on the
one hand, it does offer a symbol system for women's spiritual growth;
on the other hand, some of its views of the psyche assume an androcentric, sexist point of view. Third, women's search for a sacred image
has revealed the God/ess Within.

Women's Reality

There is no existing paradigm to express women's journey individually
or collectively, psychologically or spiritually. The story is yet to be told,
because the story is being consciously experienced in this age. That
is why the roots of our culture are now uprooted. The story we have
been told to assume as ours is that of the male hero's journey. In
its family structure and education as well as in its political, economic, and religious belief systems, our society encourages young males
to separate themselves from their families; sow some wild oats;
be self-sufficient, competitive, ambitious, and emotionally independent.
To be a man in our society requires separating yourself from your
feelings, vulnerabilities, and insecurities. By carefully structuring relationships, with roles and expectations clearly defined, a young man
gathers his strength under the guise of ultimate decision-making authority, while protecting and providing for his wife and children. He
develops a strong ego.

This scenario serves well to point out that women's experiences and
values are certainly not those experienced by men and by a society
defined by men. Nor is it helpful for those men who are working hard
to redefine maleness in something other than competitive terms. Women,

according to this story, are not expected to be concerned with ego development. Women are to be the emotional repositories for men's feelings and find their self-definition and fulfillment through their achieving male partner. Thus, "separation and sexism have functioned together as the most fundamental self-shaping assumptions of our culture."[1]

As women begin to tell their own stories, other factors, values and concerns surface as central to women's self-understanding and ego development. Given the androcentric norms for ego development, women would appear to have no ego at all. This immensely affects women's self-esteem and energy. Although women have been treated as subordinate creatures for thousands of years, this subordination has been meshed with intense and significant relationships with men and family since women are essential for the survival of the species. As subordinates, we are defined as inferior and expected to conform to the expectations of the dominant group. Characteristically, women's attitudes indicate a lack of initiative; an inability to act, decide, or think; docility; passivity; and submissiveness. These attitudes are so ingrained in our culture that a woman acting otherwise is met with subtle or even overt aggression. Therefore, for women to struggle for ego identification is *in itself* a countercultural act since women are expected to follow the male-defined norms of society. "A woman's direct action can result in a combination of economic hardship, social ostracism, and psychological isolation—and even the diagnosis of a personality disorder."[2]

Gender identification is the first statement made about humans at birth—a statement that unconsciously reinforces a culturally accepted androcentric bias reflected in societal expectations, potentialities, meaning, fulfillment, and affirmation. Without cultural support, women have come to believe and accept secondary status as their lot. Women must carry a huge psychological burden in order to be freed from this expected state of inferiority. Women must be willing to risk everything in order to ask questions, questions that cast all the assumptions of our culture regarding women and women's roles in a new light. Women's struggle for self-articulation and self-identity is the essence of the women's movement. Offering solidarity and the energy necessary to confront and expose prejudice on such a massive scale, the women's movement also provides women with the affirmation and recognition needed in self-valuation. Women realize that they cannot do it alone. Contrary to the male hero's journey, women travel together toward personal and group transformation. Thus, what we accomplish is not for ourselves alone, but for the wider culture.

Because women have so internalized their inferior status, they cannot easily or realistically see their strengths and shortcomings or understand

their confused emotional state. This "internalized inferiority"[3] has infected their self-image to such an extent that virtually "all women in
our society arrive at adulthood with significant feelings of inadequacy."[4]
Accepting these feelings as appropriate perpetuates and indeed substan-
tially contributes to women's lack of self-confidence and self-esteem.
So accustomed have women become to a lack of integral respect, that
a major task of any therapeutic process is the establishing of a sense
of personal integrity, authority, and self-esteem. Women must come
to believe in themselves, that they are worth fighting for!

Women's Ego Development

As the scapegoat for our society, "women, by their very existence,
confront and challenge men because they [women] have been made
the embodiment of the dominant culture's unsolved problems."[5] These
problems have to do with relationship—with ourselves, our intimate
relationships, our feelings, our children, our vulnerabilities, our survival
as a species and the survival of our planet. In order to meet these
needs, women are suggesting a different type of ego development by
embracing both relationship and the typical need for separation as a
model for even greater integration of human potential. "Women are
quite validly seeking something more complete than autonomy as it
is defined by men, a fuller not a lesser ability to emcompass relationships
to others, simultaneous with the fullest development of oneself."[6] Inter-
mingling the insights of psychology, sociology, and spirituality, this new
model gains significance for us today. For women, "identity and intimacy
are intricately conjoined"[7] in the living process of ego development.

Carol Gilligan affirms the significance of women's decision-making
processes that are made in conjunction with the needs of others and
one's moral responsibility to relationships. Thus, women's convictions
are grounded in the lived reality of another, not a theory of what appears
to be objectively fair as defined by individual rights and rules. "The
morality of rights differs from the morality of responsibility in its emphasis on separation rather than connection, in its consideration of the
individual rather than the relationship as primary."[8] Decisions are made
then, within a broad context, and one's ego personality—the individual—is connected to the others involved in the situation. Isolation, or
a vastly independent posture, is not really possible. Women begin this
kind of balancing of needs when they are little girls and continue through
adulthood trying to balance family needs and personal needs, child-
rearing responsibilities and career planning. Men, as yet, have had no
such demands placed on them by society. Gilligan depicts this attitudinal

shift symbolically with the images of hierarchy and the web. Women and men have differing perceptions regarding the centrality of relationships; these differences are in turn reflected in their differing concepts of self and morality as well as their modes of assertion and response. The male hierarchical model prefers competitive interactions where there are obvious winners and losers, accompanied by the fear that one day you will be replaced. The female web model desires interconnections and group dynamics with the fear of not being sufficiently related. Women's nonhierarchical vision of interdependence offers society a refreshing option to the hierarchical conflicts that plague humanity today. Nonetheless, both models are riddled with insecurities and stress, one in the area of achievement and the other in the area of affiliation:

> These disparate visions in their tension reflect the paradoxical truth of human experience—that we know ourselves as separate only insofar as we live in connection with others, and that we experience relationships only insofar as we differentiate other from self.[9]

Since women are often held accountable for their choices regarding others, women's decision-making processes can become rather complicated. In regard to themselves however, they tend to choose quickly—for the other. Women, far too frequently, under the guise of consideration and "being nice," hide their own needs and thwart their own development. Although immensely sensitive to the inclusion of others, women frequently do not include themselves. This dynamic is one of self-deception and self-deprecation. Nonetheless, "when the distinction between helping and pleasing frees the activity of taking care from the wish for approval by others, the ethic of responsibility can become a self-chosen anchor of personal integrity and strength."[10] Women are so accustomed to subordination, that they must struggle daily to articulate their needs, their views, and their presence as significant. "The language of rights underlines the importance of including in the network of care not only the other but also the self."[11]

It is just such honoring of self that causes women so much difficulty in their societal role of motherhood. Women are the mothers of the human race and "people's experience of their early relationship to their mother provides a foundation for expectations of women as mothers."[12] As Nancy Chodorow explains, however, being a mother is understood not only as birthing a child, but as providing care, nurturance, and socialization. We speak of someone "mothering" a child with this implicit understanding, be it a man or a woman. The question then becomes:

why is the person who routinely does all those activities that go into
parenting not a man? . . . Women's mothering is central to the sexual
division of labor. Women's maternal role has profound effects on women's
lives, on ideology about women, on the reproduction of masculinity and
sexual inequality, and on the reproduction of particular forms of labor
power.[13]

Conflicting relational patterns, expectations and demands from both
husband and children, lack of networking, and economic and emotional
hardship induced by a socially isolating parenting process disturb
women's inner resources and their nurturance of others and themselves.
Considerable stress revolves around the need for "normal" cultural ad-
justments of daughters and sons so that social conditioning perpetuates
imbalances and guarantees their repetition. Co-parenting might alleviate
this stress, allowing for both parents to establish personal and intimate
relationships with their children while reducing the likelihood of motherhood becoming "smotherhood" and fatherhood becoming extinct. The
establishing of better social patterns, however, requires the redefin-
ing of meaning, achievement, prestige, power, and status, along with
a societal commitment to education, economics and career-development
choices. Such revisioning depends on "the conscious organization and
activity of all women and men who recognize that their interests lie
in transforming the social organization of gender and eliminating sexual
inequality,"[14] while simultaneously encouraging each of us, parent or
not, to develop our own gifts, shared and celebrated by the community
at large.
   In summary, we can say that women's ego development and journey
story develop in unique ways that have heretofore been neither acknowledged nor understood. In the past, since women's processes were
somehow different from men's, they were interpreted as inferior and
secondary. Because we live in an age in which the search for relationships
has become important, women's ways of experiencing, relating, and
deciding have become dramatically central. Women's developmental processes offer us "the germs of a different concept of differentiation, beyond
the culture of father as differentiator, mother as that from which one
differentiates." Since women remain connected, "the oceanic feeling
of an empathic continuum initially common to both sexes . . . may
contain its own self-transforming principle of differentiation."[15] An understanding of ego development as inclusive of relationship as well as
personal autonomy offers us new models around which we may want
to make choices for our future.
   The motivating factors for the inequality of women have been fear

and insecurity that have translated into sexism in our society. However, "relation can either foster dependency, or test and nurture freedom."[16] The culture's insistence on separation as the prevailing myth accents gynophobia, especially of women who affirm a radical interconnection between persons and responsibilities that makes "the loner" no longer attractive. Since we can never grow outside of our gender identities, the cultural valuation or devaluation of gender molds and directs our psychological/spiritual growth. Thus, what we value in the human we honor in the Divine. What we devalue in the human we deny in the Divine. In this way, androcentrism dictates our religious belief system.

Jungian Observations

Much of Jungian psychology seems to offer an integrative model for women's spiritual growth. An acknowledgment of the existence of the collective unconscious connects human experience in a radical way. A symbol system that includes primordial images is capable of embracing the feminine. And an understanding of "Self" as the "Sacred Within" encourages women to continue their search for the feminine Divine. Extensive study of these and other areas is common among Jungians, whose work is often accessible to general readers. New books on Jungian psychology fill the bookstores every year.

Nonetheless, although they are gradually developing, feminist critiques are still rare among Jungians. I believe it is important for women and men to realize that some Jungian interpretations, in addition to their wealth of insight into the intricacies of the psyche, are nonetheless androcentric and sexist. Therefore I think it is appropriate to comment in a general way on the limitations as well as benefits women can expect from Jungian psychology. In this section, I will comment on the limitations I have observed. Then in the following section, "The God/ess Within," I will explore some of the beneficial insights that Jungian interpretation offers us, focusing on our search for the feminine Divine.

With regard to the limitations of Jungian psychology, I will briefly explore several areas of concern. First is the fact that the hero's journey begins with the act of matricide. Second is the subtle perpetuation of the idea that women's primary function is to serve men in their development in a nonthreatening fashion. Third is the frequent evidence of a sexist, derogatory attitude that contributes to women's poor self-image. Fourth and finally, I will comment on the general confusion over the interfacing of the lives of real women with unconscious energies. Unless we take these limitations into account, Jungian psychology generally remains at best only partially helpful; for many women it would be completely unsuitable. By briefly exploring these areas, we can see how these limitations are roadblocks to women's quest, making it even harder to experience the God/ess Within.

The First Act of the Hero's Journey Is Matricide

Aware of the dominant masculine imbalance of our culture and consciousness, Jung upheld the necessity for the integration of the feminine. "Though individuation presupposes an ego defined by separation from the mother, the whole self at which individuation aims requires ultimate reconciliation, in terms of the Jungian imagery, with the slaughtered mother."[17] Nonetheless, to insist that ego development be separatist makes the journey toward integration more cumbersome. If, as women are suggesting, ego development should align identity with relationship, then the mother would not need to be symbolically slaughtered in the first place. This mythic slaying of the mother-dragon is based on a profound fear of women and all that is feminine. Consistent with patriarchal thought, the feminine is here portrayed in dualistic terms: positive images, particularly for Christians, include Mother Church and the Virgin Mary; negative images include the Dark Abyss or Terrible Mother. The newly separated ego is in constant danger of being swallowed up by a terrible negative feminine power who must be overcome at all costs:

> It is from Jung that we learn most definitively that the mythic matricide is an act of self-defense on the part of the heroic ego consciousness and that this matricide repeats itself endlessly in a culture centered around such an ego's consciousness. . . . [In exactly this way] . . . psychic matricide conspires with interpersonal and social misogyny.[18]

Thus the story reinforces cultural bias against women as the image makers of the feminine. Furthermore, what are the implications for women to hear affirmed a journey story that insists the "first creative act of liberation is matricide,"[19] as a symbolic death-wish? If we didn't live in a patriarchal culture, would such a story ever be told? This myth is part of our culture's projection onto "the mother"—and therefore onto women. It is, however, "neither an instinctual nor an eternal necessity."[20]

Confirming that our journey story thus far is focused on the archetypal hero, James Hillman asserts the necessity for the return to the feminine "soul," or "way of being," which includes deep inner feelings, vulnerabilities, and relationships. In an interview with Barbara Dunn, Hillman suggests that an essential part of the hero myth is the fear of falling out of control and being swallowed up by the mother.

> That's because the narrative of independence that we currently believe says individuation is an Heroic journey away from the Mother. . . . Through this narrative we've set the Mother up to be grasping and clutching, because we say we must leave her. But she may be saying, "You don't have to leave me. I'm the Ground. I'm Life. I'm Nature and rocks. I'm the Earth. I'm Eternal Love. . . . The most important thing is that the Mother is whatever the Mother is. She may want to hold you forever, but you have to learn what that holding is. Her holding can be sustaining. Why must the Hero pull away, cut away from her?[21]

Because she represents elemental life force, she cannot be eliminated. But she can be accepted, and for women to even try to kill her is to kill a part of themselves. In our search for new metaphors and images, there returns to us the sacred image of the Black Madonna. Long ago rejected, her reemergence into the consciousness of so many people today reminds us of our need to reclaim "the sacredness of matter, the intersection of sexuality and spirituality." This embodied image of the feminine Divine could empower us—both women and men—to embrace an integrating and affirming sacred presence that could radicalize our inner selves and therefore our cultural assumptions. This Mother image, rather than being banished as a shadow figure to be destroyed, isolated, or feared, is resurfacing as a positive Mother figure. As Marion Woodman states,

> the world has never known Conscious Mother, let alone Conscious Mature Woman. We have to connect to her because the power that drives the patriarchy, the power that is raping the earth, the power drive behind addictions, has to be transformed.[22]

This interpretation of the significance and power of the Mother, of the feminine, is a positive step toward relinquishing the patriarchal need "to slay the dragon." As we search for soul, we search for a new myth, a new story where relatedness and personhood meet, a valuing of life here and now, on this sacred planet—a return to the feminine and the God/ess Within.

Women's Primary Function Is to Serve Men

"Man has really experienced woman only as mother, loved one, and so on, that is, always in ways related to himself."[23] This egotistical attitude, stated by Emma Jung, actually presupposes, despite knowledge to the contrary, that man (*not* in a generic sense) is indeed the center of the universe. Carl Jung in effect agreed with this stance by maintaining that woman

> takes up her position as the most immediate environmental influence in the life of the adult man. She becomes his companion, she belongs to him in so far as she shares his life and is more or less of the same age. . . . [Woman] is and always has been a source of information about things for which a man has no eyes. She can be his inspiration; her intuitive capacity, often superior to man's, can give him timely warning, and her feeling, always directed towards the personal, can show him ways which his own less personally accented feeling would never have discovered.[24]

All of these are wonderful qualities, to be celebrated and affirmed. They are also the very qualities that our culture, and an androcentric psychology, regard as inferior. Rather than affirm woman as woman, the closest we can get to affirmation is to include these womanly qualities as helpful to men and their development.

Toni Wolff made a study of the personality types of women. She called these types maternal, hetaera, amazon, and mediumistic, and described their respective relationships with men. It is interesting to note that all four personality types are defined in terms of women's relationship to men. I shall briefly comment on two: the amazon and the medium. The amazon, depicting women's sense of independence and selfhood—and therefore potentially articulating for women a posture of personal integrity and direction—is couched in negative terms because an amazon woman is not willing to be subservient to men.[25] The word *amazon* itself is loaded with negativity. A woman depicted as amazon threatens the male-defined political power of society by refusing to mold herself into dependency.

The mediumistic woman is not, however, such a threat. "Her role is still, as it always has been, to be a mediator to man of his own creative inspirations, a channel whereby the riches of the unconscious can flow to him more easily than if she were not there."[26] The assumption remains that a woman's ideal purpose for existence is as helper. As long as women accept this imposed definition, men will certainly oblige. Why have women accepted this role and how has it served them? Why are women apparently willing to channel the unconscious for men and yet are reluctant to do so for themselves? Assisting men is perfectly legitimate, but existing to be at their service is all together different—and unacceptable.

Women do, of course, function well in the world of relationships. And women have embraced this function with high energy and graciousness. We have created the gift called "home" and have united warmth and beauty with daily provision making. It is not the task of feminists to eliminate this aspect of women's awareness and sensitivity. Nonetheless, women's "chief satisfaction" as "homemakers" (defined as meeting the needs of others) empowers our culture to restrict both women's and men's familial response-abilities. Motivating women to accept this role, society simultaneously undervalues "women's work" while criticizing women's supposed lack of development.

A Sexist and Derogatory Attitude Contributes to Women's Poor Self-Image

Any theory or therapeutic process that does not confront personal and cultural internalized oppression is not only not a liberating process for women but detrimental to inner growth. In his essay "Modern Women in Europe," Jung states that man's pursuit of consciousness cannot proceed until woman's efforts toward consciousness increases. Men are more developed than women because men have defined growth in terms of a strongly defined independent ego. Jung's bias assumes that this definition is valid: because women have not developed *according to male standards,* they have not developed at all. This bias ignores the fact that women's ego development follows a different path.

> If women sustain a more lucid connection with the unconscious from the outset [which Jung proposes], this makes us not less but more conscious. For what is it to become conscious but to make intentional connection with what has previously remained unconscious? We do not need to be "masculine" as we mature, but more focused, more creative, more luminous just as women.[27]

Emma Jung states well the most common of the negative or devaluing attitudes aimed at women and their struggle in society:

> In general, it can be said that feminine mentality manifests an undeveloped, childlike, or primitive character; instead of the thirst for knowledge, curiosity; instead of judgment, prejudice; instead of thinking, imagination or dreaming; instead of will, wishing[28]

Here, women are naturally immature, "childish" creatures. This attitude encourages society's injustices that discriminate against women in the first place, adding to women's supposed negative qualities that of vicarious living, which is deadly in and of itself. Simultaneously, it disregards and devalues curiosity, imagination, and the ability to dream or envision a new reality (except, I presume, when a man is doing the envisioning).

Another Jungian assumption is that women are narcissistic. It is interesting to note that "the only socially condoned form of power openly afforded" women is in their appearance.[29] This puts women in considerable conflict. Despite society's discouragement, women prefer to be aware of their bodies, live in their bodies, and affirm their bodies. Women's pride in appearance reaffirms their sense of earth-body connection within a society where appearance and health are closely identified. But our culture, in its obsession with thinness and stereotypical sexual behavior, combines appearance and body in such a way as to undermine women's efforts at integration. While allowing women to feel "appealing" (and therefore "relate-able"), appearance as power also falls into the trap of androcentric thinking and behaving, confirming many women's mistaken belief that the only way they can relate is through their bodies.[30]

Women's Psychic Energies are Split

There is a tendency in patriarchal cultures to categorize women with two opposing images. Relevant to Jungian psychology, this is evidenced most significantly through the archetypal mother and the animus.

In much Jungian thought, mother images are held in high esteem while the lives of real women are relativized in relation to this ideal. This is complicated by the fact that the "positive" mother archetype, having been defined by patriarchy, characterizes those qualities that are necessary for survival and are therefore culturally acceptable. Other feared qualities become part of the "negative" mother archetype or perhaps are understood as animus-possession. In either case, women's energies remain split: nonunderstandable, unreal, and bothersome. Additionally, only the "positive" mother archetype becomes the male defined expectation to which real women can only partially succeed and are only partially affirmed.

The chasm between the power of the mother archetype and the lives of real women—in light of the fact that we have not affirmed a Feminine Divine Presence within our spiritual practices—offers complicated mixed messages. After extensive honoring of the mother archetype, Jung comments on women themselves:

Why risk saying too much about the human being who was our mother, the accidental carrier of the great experience which includes herself and myself and all [hu]mankind, and indeed the whole of created nature, the experience of life whose children we are?[31]

While Jung may have intended to relieve women from responsibility because of the significance and intensity of the archetypal energy, women are nonetheless relativized, considered only marginally significant, regarded as merely "accidental" to the co-creation and birthing of all humanity. What appears to be more important to Jung is the archetype, *per se*, as a noncorporal energy of the psyche, thus emphasizing a mind/body split. Jung does concede that "a man's statements about the mother are always emotionally prejudiced,"[32] and that because the mother symbol is immensely powerful to a man, he tries to idealize her. Nonetheless, "[i]dealization is a hidden apotropaism; one idealizes whenever there is a secret fear to be exorcized,"[33] and it is this fear that is projected onto women.

Additionally, much of contemporary Jungian understanding of the animus as an element in women's psyche is prejudicial, the theory supporting even the existence of the animus is androcentric. Jung's theories rest on pairs of opposites, and because he posited the anima in the experiences of men, he concluded that women's psyche must include an animus. Sounding somewhat surprised, Jung states: "But I have, as a rule, found it very difficult to make a woman understand what the animus is, and I have never met any woman who could tell me anything definite about his personality."[34] Rather than modify the theory to fit reality, Jungians have held tight to Jung's theory and required women to adjust. Just what are women supposed to do?

As women's unconscious contrasexual energy, the animus refers to women's ways of making judgments. "The animus-ridden woman is ruled by preconceived notions, prejudices and expectations, is dogmatic, argumentative and overgeneralizing."[35] Jung's descriptions of the animus process is also decidedly negative. Describing, as he says, "one of these creatures" (a woman), he includes the following qualifiers: harping, irrelevant, weak, nonsensical, tangled up, maddening, perverse, exasperating the man.[36] A more subtle abuse of women than the theory of penis envy, the animus has been surrounded with negativity, epitomized by Jung's statement: "A woman possessed by the animus is always in danger of losing her femininity."[37] Women have been accused of not knowing how to think and decide, and are told that if they identify with the animus they risk their feminine identity, which only furthers women's woundedness. Nonetheless, in theory at least, a woman needs her animus—her "inner man"—to develop her thinking, rational, focused capacities. However,

> By conceptualizing their thinking side as masculine, women are distanced from their thinking. To be more precise, if a woman refers to her "thinking side" as "he," personifying it in Jungian fashion, she colludes with a patriarchally encouraged tendency to see only the male as rational, logical, and dependable. Just as men need to own their *male* vulnerability, dependency, and fears of embodiment, so do women need to own their *female* authority, clarity, and analytical ability and in this way challenge and help to break down patriarchal society's fear of authority in women.[38]

These observations have focused on some of the limitations of Jungian interpretation. But there remains a great deal of positive insight for women's search for meaning and integration. In the following section, I will explore some of the images, myths, and religious symbols that are particularly helpful to women.

The God/ess Within

Jungian psychology is one of the psychological systems to take seriously the human search for the Divine. There are many spiritual undertones and overtones in Jungian archetypal imagery, particularly in the concept of the Self as the God/ess Within, that offer us an intimate and sustaining grounding for our lives, a rootedness in the deep mysteries which we have called "The Holy." Jung would not deny that his system gives considerable attention to "the sacred" through its use of symbol.[39] Jung also held the view that, as contemporary religious institutions collapse, "new images, symbols, and myths emerge from the collective unconscious to take their place" through the "religious function" of the human psyche. "Without this function humans cannot survive, for humans cannot live without meaning."[40] Thus, the purpose of religion is to bind together and connect our lives, to support us through the perils of life and death in a meaningful way.

The mother-daughter relationship, common to all women, is an appropriate religious symbol as women reimagine themselves as full participants in the Divine Presence. How can the mother inside each of us, who is both grieved and enraged by oppression, transform the prison of oppression for the daughter inside each of us? With the resurrection of the daughter an alteration of patriarchal consciousness becomes possible. The bonding of women, as women, propels us to a unity of life and blood that, when empowered within us, unites all femaleness—

daughters, mothers, the earth herself. Such strength, integrity, and assertion of cosmic connection are capable of transforming our culture, and
thus of rescuing our planet. The symbols and power for this process
of re-membering the feminine Divine can be found in various sources,
among them the Greek Goddesses, the story of the descent of Inanna,
the image of the Blessed Virgin Mary, and in woman as a sacred symbol.

The Greek Goddesses

"A myth is like a dream that we recall even when it is not understood,
because it is symbolically important."[41] The stories of the Greek Goddesses portray inner energy patterns that are symbolically true to our
experience. The Greek Goddesses, because they play out patterns of
behavior in women's lives, provide us with insight and meaning. These
Goddesses are considered archetypal, that is, they reflect unconscious
inner images that are expressed in much of our behavior. The patterns
exhibited by the Goddesses are common to many women and are therefore expressive of collective female experience, transcending individual
responses. Their power in our lives, therefore, becomes like a godly
power, putting us in touch with inner numinous energies, symbolic
of that which is otherwise unexpressed or unnoticed. Each of the Goddesses can represent inner energy patterns available to women in search
of deeper self-understanding and relationship to the feminine Divine.
(All of these Goddesses, in various ways, parallel the Great Goddess—
Inanna—whom we will consider in the next section.) As told in a patriarchal Greek culture, the stories of these Goddesses are limited to certain
realms and are not able to influence all aspects of human behavior.
Nonetheless, they all require our due respect.[42]

In her book *Goddesses in Everywoman,* Jean Shinoda Bolen explores
the significance of the Goddesses in the lives of contemporary women.[43]
She has grouped the Goddesses according to general energy patterns
or functions in women's lives. The first group is the virgin Goddesses:
Artemis, Athena, and Hestia. They represent the at-one-ness qualities
women enjoy—an inner sense of self-sufficiency, independence, and pur-
posefulness. They are neither victimized by others nor dominated by
patriarchal society. They have learned how to cope with patriarchy,
how to be their own person, how to focus their energies on what is
personally significant. They might be considered today as "father's
daughters," women oriented toward achievement and nonemotional involvement. These Goddesses express women's need for self-direction
and autonomy. These qualities are being recognized today due to the
emergence of women's consciousness (although the archetype of the

"independent woman" has not yet been sufficiently honored in traditional Jungian thought).

The second group of Goddesses Bolen calls the vulnerable Goddesses: Hera, Persephone, and Demeter. These Goddesses represent women's inner drive for relationship and affiliation. These parts of woman's experience expose her to achieving a sense of security and purpose vicariously, generally through her male partner. Overidentification with these Goddesses in our androcentric society has humiliated women, encouraging their subservience, domination, and codependency. Nonetheless, women experience firsthand the importance of relationship and intimacy and they value these aspects of human life in community. Simultaneously, through these Goddesses' myths, women can come to know the painful sufferings and losses frequently evident in relationships today.

Bolen's third category is made up of only one Goddess, Aphrodite, the Goddess of love and beauty. She is that aspect of women's experience that generates sensuality, sexuality, and erotic attraction. Aphrodite, however, is a virgin, that is, a woman unto herself, because she was never victimized through her liaisons. She entered and left relationships of her own choosing. Thus, she maintained her own independence, but because she was in relationship she was able to be vulnerable, to enjoy beauty and sensuality. Women learn about their own eroticism and creative energies through Aphrodite with an increased willingness to risk and change.[44]

The qualities of these Goddesses appear to be inherent in many women, causing conflict and confusion, crisis and growth. In honoring these inner Goddesses, with their respective strengths and weaknesses, women can learn more and more about their individual needs and responsibilities. The Goddesses can become metaphors or symbols of the multidimensional aspects of women's concerns and provide a lens for clarification and decision making. Also, since these Goddesses are adapted to a patriarchal life and culture, they can model that process for many women striving to do the same in a similar culture today. While certain aspects of certain Goddesses exert more or less power in a woman's psyche, an integration becomes possible by imaging these godly powers within. By invoking these Goddesses women can avail themselves of this power and presence.

> Athena, help me to think clearly in this situation.
> Persephone, help me to stay open and receptive.
> Hera, help me to make a commitment and be faithful.
> Demeter, teach me to be patient and generous, help me to be a good mother.

Artemis, keep me focused on that goal in the distance.
Aphrodite, help me to love and enjoy my body.
Hestia, honor me with your presence, bring me peace and serenity.[45]

The Descent of Inanna

The ancient Sumerian myth of the Great Goddess Inanna is, in fact,
an earlier female version of the Christ myth. Sylvia Brinton Perera provides a brilliant in-depth study of it in her book *Descent to the Goddess*.
As the Goddess of the Great Above, Inanna requests to visit the "land
of no return" in order to attend to the funeral of Gugalanna, husband
of Ereshkigal, the Goddess of the Great Below. Inanna is required to
submit to the dark, to descend into hell, to bear the burden of deprivation
and uselessness so that "there is no way out of the despair. [She] can
only endure, barely conscious, barely surviving the pain and powerless-
ness, suspended out of life, stuck, until and if, some act of grace with
some new wisdom arrives."[46] Women and men need to be mindful of
this dark place of purification.

In this story it is not the terrible mother who is killed but rather
the Goddess of Light who is sacrificed—made holy—through the darkness. In the Goddess tradition, darkness is not associated with evil
and sin. And so, like the Christ myth, this story empowers not by
abandoning the darkness, but by going through it. However, unlike
the Christian myth as it is generally taught and believed, there is no
expiation for sin. Inanna's journey is not to redeem us from sin, but
to embrace the fullness of life in all its demonic aspects. There is no
conquering over death. Rather, death and life are reunited. Darkness
is not assumed to be the enemy. The Great Below "simply demands
recognition as a power equal to that of the Great Above."[47] Ereshkigal
kills Inanna and hangs her body on a peg for three days like a piece
of rotting meat. When Inanna is rescued by two little insignificant
mourners sent from above, Ereshkigal is neither overpowered nor made
to bow low in any way. Ereshkigal allows the release of her dead sister
because the mourners commiserate with her, empathizing with her pain.
Ereshkigal is transformed through their compassion and Inanna's dead
body is permitted passage to the Great Above, where she lives once
again. Inanna, realizing that this encounter with her dark powerful
shadow sister brings altogether new levels of consciousness, requires
her consort Dumuzi to travel to the dark abyss as well.[48]

This powerful story is a journey to the Great Mother. In our culture
we have all been undermothered. We have been so influenced by patriarchy that we undervalue that which mothers us, the Great Mother Within,

who affirms and gives birth to our wholeness. As women of our time, we are being provoked into letting go of our identifications with a patriarchal society. We must let go of ourselves as daughters of the patriarchy and re-member ourselves as daughters of the Great Goddess "because so much of the power and passion of the feminine has been dormant in the underworld—in exile for five thousand years." But even in this retelling of the story, the Great Goddess is split in two, thus necessitating the journey for unification and integration with fully embodied female images. Inanna becomes the first to model the journey to the deep in search of feminine wisdom through this act of at-one-ness. This connection is vital to women's journey today, evidenced by an active willingness to be open to experiences of the numinous. "This myth shows us also how those dark, repressed levels may be raised, and how they may enter conscious life—through emotional upheavals and grief—to radically change conscious energy patterns."[49]

It is important to realize that Inanna was a powerful Goddess. And yet, "in spite of her power as goddess [sic] of fertility, order, war, love, the heavens, healing, emotions, and song; in spite of having the titles Lady of Myriad Offices and Queen, Inanna is a wanderer." She is betrayed by patriarchy and leaves in search of Self, as women are doing today. Ereshkigal, too, originated in the Above as the grain Goddess. She represents "The Great Round" of nature, the seed dying to birth, the sprout dying to birth, the fruit dying to birth. Women, allies of human birthing, know the intrinsic death/life interconnection as one primary energy. To patriarchy, however, death destroys life, is something to be feared, controlled, and overcome. Ereshkigal represents that which has been rejected by patriarchy: undifferentiated primal energy and raw instinctuality, the preethical law of reality and the immensely slow hidden creativity of matter. And she requires complete submission to personal and cosmic evolution. Here we meet ourselves, perhaps for the first time.[50]

By hanging on the peg of unconsciousness, we become filled with feminine inner strength, allowing ourselves, through this ordeal, to realize and claim our own potency. The two sister Goddesses, journeying together, create the pattern for the mother-daughter biunity of the Great Goddess, portraying a wholeness for the feminine Self where both aspects of the Goddess are honored and acclaimed.[51] Thus, the closer our identification with patriarchy, the more concretely women's connection to the sacred, as expressed by the God/ess Within, becomes diminished. And it is exactly this God/ess Within whom we are called to embrace.

The Blessed Virgin Mary

The process of re-membering the feminine Divine is symbolized in the Christian tradition by the Virgin Mother Mary. Devotion to Mary has a long and intense history in Catholic circles. The official church however, presents such a male version of a sterile female, that, as I stated earlier, some feel her image is beyond repair. Doctrinally, she is not acknowledged for her divinity nor is she allowed to be fully human as a model of female personhood that is vibrant, decisive, integral, and compassionate. Central as she is, Mary's official place in Christianity fails to come even close to the mystery she truly represents, unconsciously understood by peoples of numerous cultures and expressed by extensive rituals honoring her as Goddess. Since the Second Vatican Council Mary has been severely "demoted" from her position of centrality in the worship practices of the people, especially in the United States. And without this projected female image, badly represented as it was, the unconscious has reactivated its energy, searching for an appropriate image to honor. In this search, feminists have realized that

> behind her sanitized figure lurk all the great pagan goddesses of the ancient world. Like Persephone, goddess of the underworld, Mary intercedes on behalf of the dead. Like the earth goddesses Cybele, Gaia and Demeter, Mary is prior to God and forms the ground of His being. Like the virgins—Athena and Artemis—Mary is free from bonds of marriage to mortal men. Mary derives her power in the fact that she compels minds and hearts from the vestiges of these vibrant goddesses she was supposed to replace.[52]

In the terminology of Jungian psychology we would say that deep within the collective unconscious are *a priori* archetypal energies that contain our experiences of the Divine. Erich Neumann concurs that the symbolic expression of this psychic energy "is to be found in the figures of the great goddesses represented in the myths and artistic creations of [hu]mankind."[53] As women and men search today for life-giving symbols, Mary embodies the feminine so obviously missing from the current Christian belief system.

Jung held the belief that the proclamation of the Assumption of Mary as dogma in the Catholic church was of special significance to this quest:

> the relationship to the earth and to matter is one of the inalienable qualities of the mother archetype. So that when a figure that is conditioned by

this archetype is represented as having been taken up into heaven, the realm of the spirit, this indicates a union of earth and heaven, or of matter and spirit. . . .

Understood concretely, the Assumption is the absolute opposite of materialism. Taken in this sense, it is a counterstroke that does nothing to diminish the tension between the opposites, but drives it to extremes.

Understood symbolically, however, the Assumption of the body is a recognition and acknowledgement of matter, which in the last resort was identified with evil only because of an overwhelmingly "pneumatic" tendency in man. . . . The "psychization" of matter [that is inherent consciousness] puts the absolute immateriality of spirit in question, since this would have to be accorded a kind of substantiality. The dogma of the Assumption. . . . [symbolically] has the great advantage of being able to unite heterogeneous or even incommensurable factors in a *single* image.[54]

The Assumption of Mary then, is the honoring of the sacred nature of matter—most appropriately, in female form. Teilhard and post-Teilhardian physicists, cosmologists, historians, and religious leaders reiterate for us the impact of this revelation on the human sphere.[55] Mary, symbolically for all of us, indeed for the universe, embodies this eternal union.

Artistic expression has long been understood as a medium for the unconscious. Artwork depicting, for example, the coronation of Mary as Queen of Heaven frequently presents her as God/ess returning home to the Divine. Perhaps the artists had no such intention. Nonetheless, medieval iconography "evolved a quaternity symbol in its representations of the coronation of the Virgin and surreptitiously put it in the place of the Trinity."[56] This inclusion of the Blessed Mother Mary represents an absolute time-space materiality as the realization of the fourth dimension of the Trinity.[57] However, even though this doctrine affirms the sacredness of creation depicted in female form, Mary is not understood to be God/ess "from the beginning," and thus her part in the Divine Unity is not fully acknowledged. It is precisely this point that keeps her in her place; she is not of divine origin. This is a major reason why Mary has not been able to meet the needs of some Christian feminists in search of the feminine Divine. Although she holds within her symbolically much of what is necessary for us to know her as Divine, doctrinally she fails.[58] Paradoxically, according to Jung, the doctrine of the *Assumptio Mariae* initiates this process, if not theologically, then psychologically. His interpretation allows for the inclusion of corporeality within divinity. Jung concludes:

The admission of the *Beata Virgo* is a daring attempt, in so far [*sic*] as she belongs to *lubricum illud genus* ("that slippery sex"—St. Epipanius), so suspect to the moralistic propensities of the said Church. However, she has been spiritually "disinfected" by the dogma of *Conceptio Immaculata*. I consider the Assumption as a cautious approach to the solution of the problem of opposites, namely, to the integration of the fourth metaphysical figure into the divine totality. The Catholic Church has almost succeeded in creating a quaternity without shadow, but the devil is still outside. The Assumption is at least, an important step forward in Christian (?) symbolism. This evolution will be completed when the dogma of the Co-Redemptrix is reached. But the main problem will not be solved although one pair of opposites has been smuggled into the divine wholeness.[59]

The unresolved "main problem" is the exclusion of the unconscious Shadow, or the Inanna/Ereshkigal unity previously described: traditional Christian God-talk includes only that which is accepted as "eternally good."

Woman as Sacred Symbol

Woman herself can be considered a sacred symbol. Woman is the symbol of the sacred body from which we all come, "the first and most basic experience of the feminine."[60] The holy work of birthing identifies woman with the cosmic cycle of birth, death, and rebirth celebrated in the blood mysteries. Erich Neumann reminds us that

> whenever we encounter the symbol of rebirth we have to do with a matriarchal transformation mystery; and this is true even when its symbolism or interpretation bear a patriarchal disguise.[61]

Symbolically then, even if denied by patriarchal religion, woman is the life-vessel, the one who creates, gives birth to life and sends it out into the world. Although not well understood in the religious practices of our day, the vessel symbol appears "even at the highest level as the vessel of spiritual transformation"[62] exemplified by the cup of lifeblood at the Last Supper.

Pre-Christian plunge baths re-membered the Great Mother, the life-giving womb associated with the waters of new life. This living water was translated in Christianity into the words whereby Christ identified himself as Eternal Living Water—which may in turn be seen as being drawn from the well deep within the earth, the womb from which rebirth is accomplished through the Spirit (*Ruah*), the feminine presence of God.

For a woman, this transforming process does not happen outside of her, or next to her, but within her embodied Self:

> the symbols of the transformative character almost always retain a connection with the elementary character of the Feminine and with the symbols of the womb and belly region. In direct correspondence with the symbolism of the body-vessel, the upper is built on the lower and is inconceivable except in connection with it. The transformation starts at the lower level and encompasses it. In the matriarchal world it is never a free-floating, rootless, "upper" process, as the abstract male intellect typically imagines. . . . But the maternal water not only contains; it also nourishes and transforms, since all living things build up and preserve their existence with the water or milk of the earth.[63]

In a matriarchal consciousness, it is woman who creates, nourishes, and sustains life; it is woman who gives birth not only to her own likeness—femaleness—but to "the other," maleness. This "original form of consciousness" is more open to the unconscious and consciously more receptive to it as well. Patriarchal consciousness is usually more detached and distinct. Both awarenesses however are central to any creative work.[64]

As primary life giver, woman has celebrated the sacred rites as priestess. As Neumann points out, sacred transformation "can only be effected by the woman because she herself, in her body that corresponds to the Great Goddess, is the caldron of incarnation, birth, and rebirth."[65] Furthermore, each woman can experience this transformation within herself as she is drawn to be more and more aware of the blood mysteries of her own body.

The power behind the experience of bleeding is that women are enabled to enter into the deep mysteries of life while learning to endure, to submit to the dark that is beyond conscious human control, and to learn that the way of life giving, physically as well as spiritually, comes from within. Women know—in the deep sense of knowing, not limited to the rationality of left-brain discursive thought—that life and death are one, that there is a time to embrace and a time to let go. And they know that new life comes from within not from without, transforming even as you are transformed, body from body, in vibrant life connection. Women learn in their journey to be with mystery—perceiving that something inside of us dies and we must attend to its burial—cultivating an attitude of conversion so that healing is possible. The return to the archetypal feminine embraces this great and terrible goddess as life force. "Hanging in there" on Ereshkigal's meat hook is not passive submission but freely and actively choosing, creating, awaiting, birthing, celebrating new life.

Blood is a divine fluid, numinous and empowering, and the special possession of woman. If a man is to enter into this sanctuary he must be deeply in touch with his "feminine within," symbolized by his being dressed as a woman.[66] In Christian liturgies today, where women are sometimes marginalized or prohibited from presiding because of a mixture of fear and awe of these blood mysteries, male shamans, the priests, must dress like women as a symbol of reaching down into the unconscious, their femaleness, to be in touch with the numinous.

The God/ess Within as a vessel of the sacred is frequently depicted in Christian artwork. A fifteenth-century wood sculpture, the *Vierge Ouvrante,* depicts the mother and child so familiar in Catholic churches. When a container in the sculpture is opened, the mystery the Virgin holds for us is revealed as a "heretical secret within her." God the Father and God the Son, almighty lords high above the earth, who "in an act of pure grace raise up the humble, earth-bound mother to abide with them, prove to be contained in her; prove to be 'contents' of her all-sheltering body."[67] Another example of this theme, although considerably less prominent, is represented in the painting *Saint Anne with Virgin and Child,* which demonstrates the female intergenerational unity of the Great Mother birthing the Daughter who births the Divine Child.[68]

In discovering, as if for the first time in our age, the underpinnings of our religious stirrings in the symbol of woman, once again we are free to embrace womankind as our returning home to the Sacred Within. We discover what the

> primordial [hu]man experienced through an overpowering intuition; namely, that in the generating and nourishing, protective and transformative, feminine power of the unconscious, a wisdom is at work that is infinitely superior to the wisdom of [the hu]man's waking consciousness, and that, as source of vision, and symbol, of ritual, law and poetry, intervenes, summoned or unsummoned, to save [the hu]man and give direction to [our] life.[69]

As women intimately involved in life-giving mysteries expressed through our very bodies, we come to a deeper understanding of Self as Sacred Presence. Knowing ourselves as persons of dignity and vessels of holiness, we are encouraged to hold on to our path of connectedness, where integrity, strength, and compassion surely meet.

Chapter Three

The Goddess

It is as though we suffer from chronic amnesia. Our human story has been erased, made invisible, due to historic nearsightedness, while the misinterpretation of data has encouraged our forgetfulness. We have forgotten the prehistory of the Goddess tradition that marks the evolving religious consciousness of our species. The Goddess tradition was the first recognition of Divinity, understandably acknowledged as female. This inclination to the female and/or feminine—from a time when life was lived, experienced, and expressed in other than androcentric terms— is incredible to the patriarchal mind. There continues to be a strong resistance to taking our prehistory seriously, as though to render it impotent through general negativity, disbelief or an apparent need for "proof." To some, that the Goddess tradition could ever have existed simply boggles the mind as well as the heart!

The prehistory I refer to traces human civilizations back to the early artwork of 30,000 B.C. However, of greatest interest to us will be the archeological finds of the Neolithic-Chalcolithic period (circa 7000 to 3500 B.C.) While analysis of this material in the past has served to reinforce cultural and androcentric bias, the advance of alternate interpretations (as, for example, in the work of Marija Gimbutas) allows for an articulation of a powerful new human expression of prehistory. There are many reasons why these new insights have not yet been uniformly accepted. However, before elaborating on these, I will present some of the major advances that have indeed been made.

To enter into the experience of those who lived almost ten thousand years ago is awesomely difficult. Understandably, their lives were significantly different from our own. But that difference is not only social or developmental. It is psychic; it is spiritual. Clearly these ancient peoples lived a numinous life. Their sculptures, vases, and carvings depict a value system abundant with religious imagery and symbol. They were aware of sacred life-energy emanating from rocks and trees, from birds and serpents, from woman as life giver, from the earth herself. Numinous living does not allow dualisms to separate meaningless air from sacred breath, or to separate death from life. At night they knew they were entering sacred darkness; when they entered a cave, they knew they were entering the womb. When they tilled the soil, they knew the earth as holy. They knew these things not with our scientific minds, but with their shamanic souls. They lived in the power of the Cosmic Spirit and knew Her to be the Mother of All.

The gap between their lives and ours is almost insurmountable for many of us today: our physical selves and our spiritual selves, our outer and our inner, are radically split asunder and are generally experienced as two separate entities (when our inner self is experienced consciously at all!). There is, as it were, a hole in our psyche that is hungry for a deeply spiritual life that can breathe freely within our bodies and within the body of our earth. Returning to the Goddess, then, is not simply an intellectual task with a verifiable outcome. To return to the Goddess is to be open to Her female power and presence, to death as an aspect of life, to a cosmology that supports our relationship with the earth and all species as one breathing organism.

For those of us strongly influenced by monotheism, the oneness of the Goddess, who is expressed with such diversity among so many cultures, may not be apparent. We have the mistaken tendency to think of the Goddess as though she were many goddesses, similar to the Greek deity stories. But Joseph Campbell, mythologist and religious historian, speaks of the multiplicity within the Goddess tradition as "syncretism." The Goddess is polytheistic because She appears cross-culturally under different aspects with different names and a variety of dialects. Her aspects simply cannot be subsumed under one title, and yet, within Her diversity, She remains One. "We can properly speak of faith in the Goddess in the same way we speak of faith in [the] God as a transcending entity."[1] She is the Original Blessed Trinity—much expanded and more freely expressed (I will elaborate on this triune aspect more fully later).

As we begin to explore together our return to the Goddess, let us do so not with our minds only, but with the awareness that we stand on the sacred ground of our ancestors whose wisdom goes before us. Perhaps if we can remain open, the Goddess may live once again.

In the Beginning

Marija Gimbutas, author of *The Goddesses and Gods of Old Europe 6500–3500 B.C.*, realizing the impact of our distorted historical perspective, coined the term "Old Europe" to distinguish the Neolithic and Copper Age pre-Indo-European civilization from the Indo-Europeanized Europe of the Bronze Age. These two cultures clashed ideologically in recurring waves of invasions during the fourth millennium B.C. "Old Europe" refers to southeastern Europe's first civilization: "The first was matrifocal, sedentary, peaceful, art loving, earth- and sea-bound; the second was patrifocal, mobile, warlike, ideologically sky oriented, and indifferent to art."[2] The sophistication of the communities of Old Europe is evidenced through the formation of villages, various craft specializations for both ornamentation and tools, a rudimentary script, social governance, and the creation of religious art symbols within a viable cosmology.

> If one defines civilization as the ability of a given people to adjust to its environment and to develop adequate arts, technology, script, and social relationships it is evident that Old Europe achieved a marked degree of success.[3]

The religious life of these early peoples is, in part, enviable. Their cosmogonical and cosmological images supported a religious symbol system that expressed the inner psychic reality of the Immanent Divine. Rituals, clay models of temples or shrines, masks, and thousands of figurines and vases depict representations dedicated to the Great Goddess as the Bird or Snake Goddess and the Vegetation Goddess.[4]

The Great Goddess of Life, Death, and Regeneration

The Mother Goddess, sometimes called the Fertility Goddess, is the cosmic life-force principle. She is an integrated image influenced by both the preagricultural and agricultural eras, including aspects of what now is usually considered two opposing forces: the Lady of the Beasts, who governs the fecundity of animals, and the Terrible Mother of wild nature. During the agricultural era She was known as the Great Goddess of Life, Death, and Regeneration, or the Moon Goddess, embracing the multiplicity of feminine nature and power. "She was the giver of life and all that promotes fertility, and at the same time she was the wielder of the destructive powers of nature. The feminine nature, like the moon, is light as well as dark."[5]

Models of the Great Goddess have been depicted as the Neolithic "virgin" of the seventh-millennium sculptures from Catal Hüyük in central Anatolia and sixth-millennium goddess figurines of central Anatolia, the Aegean area and the Balkan peninsula. During this era Her head is "phallus-shaped suggesting her androgynous nature, and its derivation from Palaeolithic [*sic*] times." Divine bisexuality reinforced Her absolute power. The separation of female and male attributes seems to have occurred during the sixth millennium B.C. Five clay female sculptures (circa 6300 B.C.) have also been found in northern Greece, in a building that appears to be a shrine. Large figurines (circa 4500 B.C.) from Bulgaria portray the Great Goddess as the magician-mother. "Through the act of engraving an enormous triangle in the center of the sculpture the artist perhaps visualized the universal womb, the inexhaustible source of life, to which the dead returns in order to be born again." Buried in the fetal position in a womb, a *pithos,* were small containers filled with red color, signifying the blood needed for the restoration to new life. Death, the aspect of the Terrible Mother, was never separated from life-giving images, invoked in burial rites

> to stimulate and perpetuate the procreative powers of the deceased. The European Great Goddess, like the Sumerian Ninkhursag, gave life to the Dead (another name for Ninkhursag was *Nintinugga,* ("She who gives life to the Dead"). Her magical hands and music were for the release of the life forces.[6]

The life-giving Great Goddess appears in various parts of the world and is stylized with great consistency. Reliefs of this Goddess, with arms upraised and legs widely parted in a birthing posture, have been found in shrines, on vases and other pottery of the sixth millennium B.C. in Anatolia, Yugoslavia, Hungary, Germany, and Bohemia. So common was this image, with its life-giving sacred significance, the parted legs and pubic triangle, resembling the letter *m,* became the ideogram of the Great Goddess. Frequently this Goddess symbol was accompanied with bulls heads or horns to signify Her power, and was surrounded by magical snakes or toads.[7]

Another motif of the Great Goddess is the butterfly, frequently portrayed as the "double axe." This Goddess emblem was widespread in Minoan and Mycenaean art and religion. It also appears on Catal Hüyük frescoes and Neolithic pots. Actually, the butterfly emblem precedes the presence of metal axes by several thousand years. However, with the increasing importance of the axe during the second millennium B.C., it assimilated the image of the butterfly, becoming the "double axe."[8]

The Bird and Snake Goddess

The Goddess of the waters and of air, sometimes depicted as a bird and other times as a snake, is represented as a single divinity or as separate figures. This Old European multiple symbolism testifies to the fact that the Snake Goddess and the Bird Goddess are intricately connected.[9] Inspired by the water bird and the water snake—"the rippling of water, the sinuous movement of the snake, or a dance imitating water birds"—Paleolithic artists linked these divine symbols. Consistent with Upper Paleolithic style, the water-bird divinity was bisexual. This bisexuality may be the result of the union of two aspects—bird and snake—and is not necessarily connected to female and male aspects. The Old Europeans also created maternal images from the water and air divinities of the Snake and Bird Goddess. "A divinity who nurtures the world with moisture, giving rain, the divine food which metaphorically was also understood as mother's milk, naturally became a nurse or mother." She is the feminine principle. This maternal image is "encountered at various periods and in many regions of Old Europe, and in Minoan, Cypriote, and Mycenaean culture as well. This is exemplified by the Dimini seated Nurse or Mother, striped like a snake and with a spiralling snake over the abdomen, from the site of Sesklo," Thessaly. Her appearance as a snake or bird, with numinous eyes, demonstrates Her life-generating cosmic forces. As a woman, she is depicted as the Egyptian Great Goddess Nut, who represented the flowing unity of celestial primordial waters. In Her owl representation, She evokes death aspects.[10]

The Pregnant Vegetation Goddess

Agrarian society naturally related earth's fertility with women's fertility as the combined power of the Pregnant Vegetation Goddess. Depictions of nude pregnant women in figurines of the seventh and sixth millennia B.C. differ from those of the fifth and fourth millennia, which are "exquisitely clothed except for the abdomen, which is exposed and on which lies a sacred snake. . . . some figurines take the form of bottle-shaped amulets or rattles. . . . necessary in magical proceedings to obtain fecundity." The sacred animal of the Vegetation Goddess is the pig, whose sculptures have been found in all parts of Neolithic Old Europe. The pig's rapid growth and "soft fats apparently came to symbolize the earth itself, causing the pig to become a sacred animal probably no later than 6000 B.C." Goddess figurines wearing a pig mask "imply that the pig was a double of the Pregnant Vegetation Goddess and was her sacrificial animal."

Related to the Goddess of Vegetation are groups of interconnected symbols from the same period that represent "a male stimulating principle in nature without whose influence nothing would grow and thrive." This is symbolized by the phallus or cylinder and by an ithyphallic animal-masked man, perhaps as a goat or bull. Shrines of Catal Huyuk, some depicting androgynous figurines and other phallic symbols, are found throughout Old Europe, particularly in Neolithic Greece and Yugoslavia. Many of these figurines are decorated, some with marks of circumcision, others with snakes. "Wine cups" with phallus-shaped stems have been found, some with two heads of snakes or frogs appearing on top, human facial features or heads, or geometric designs. Other discoveries of phallic representation are stands with human or animal facial characteristics. "Some have human facial features and female breasts; others have male genitals. . . . The combining of female and male characteristics in one figurine did not completely die out after the sixth millennium B.C."[11] Later in Greek and other Old European cultures, it became known as the male god Dionysus. During these times, Dionysiac festivals included processions of huge phalli. "Dionysus was a bull-god, god of annual renewal, imbued with all the urgency of nature. Brimming with virility, he was the god most favored by women." Originally however, the male aspect was celebrated through the birth of the Divine Child, who represented the perpetuation of life. The Goddess feeding her young was the most traditional motif among agrarian religious images.[12]

We have seen how the religious beliefs of the ancient peoples are depicted through various artistic works. According to Gimbutas, there are essentially two basic symbolic categories: the first is related to water and animals, particularly the snake and the bird; the second is related to the natural cycle of the earth and moon, to the seasons and the vegetal life cycle, and to the natural life/death cycle that fills our reality. Many figurines depicting the cyclic returning and renewal of life were dedicated to the Great Goddess, the Bird or Snake Goddess, and the Vegetation Goddess with the Male God. Rituals, using these figurines, dramatized the community's concern with life and death, depicting the continuous striving toward wholeness that is the active process of creation that includes many dyings, for "the process of creation and destruction is the basis for immortality."[13] A central theme for the renewal of life was the celebration of the birth of the Child, involving the masked goddesses and the male god as related to the Vegetation Goddess.

The Old European religious beliefs did not separate the female and male principles; rather, they existed side by side, or were expressed bisexually as evidenced through various sculptures.

> The male divinity in the shape of a young man or a male animal appears to affirm and strengthen the forces of the creative and active female. Neither is subordinate to the other; by complementing one another, their power is doubled.

The Old European and Minoan cultures reflected these religious practices in their social development. With the affirmation of the Goddess came the affirmation of women who were not subject to men but rather created a "structure in which all resources of human nature, feminine and masculine, were utilzied to the full as a creative force." Although greatly distorted in the Indo-European and Greek worlds, the Old European world view influenced Western civilization more than has been acknowledged.

> European civilization was not created in the space of a few centuries (as if beginning with the Greeks); the roots are deeper—by six thousand years. That is to say, vestiges of the myths and artistic concepts of Old Europe, which endured from the seventh to the fourth millennium B.C. were transmitted to the modern Western world and became part of its cultural heritage.[14]

The Goddess Cross-Culturally

The presence of the Goddess offers us three significant aspects not available to women and men today.

> [1.] The Goddess is divine female, a personification who can be invoked in prayer and ritual; [2.] the Goddess is symbol of the life, death, and rebirth of energy in nature and culture, in personal and communal life; and [3.] the Goddess is symbol of the affirmation of the legitimacy and beauty of female power.[15]

This Goddess tradition affected many cultures and was experienced in diverse ways. Although Her stories, after thousands of centuries, are difficult to trace and frequently infected with patriarchy, to name Her as She was known in various cultures can in itself impress us with the truth of Her being. In *Ancient Mirrors of Womanhood*, by Merlin Stone, are three such stories: "Mu Olokukurtilisop," from the Cuna people of Panama; "Hsi Ho," from the Chinese culture; and

"Ala," from the Ibo people of Nigeria. Each excerpt includes Stone's introductory remarks.[16]

Mu Olokukurtilisop

> Knowledge of the puberty rituals for young women, and the rever-
> ence for the Goddess, of the Cuna peoples of Panama, is drawn
> from anthropological field studies done during this century, espe-
> cially the work of Dr. Clyde Keeler. The painting of the red juice
> of the saptur fruit upon the face of the initiate, as a symbol of
> the menarche, is echoed in menarche rituals among the Navajo.
> The cave, as the burial place of the dead, offers an interesting
> parallel to the womb/cave of the Goddess as Kunapipi in Australia.

Deep in the sacred caves of the mountain Tarcarcuna, overlooking the deep waters of the Gulf of Darien, the spirit of the Goddess Mu, Giant Blue Butterfly Lady, still lingers lovingly, protecting the women of the Cuna tribe.

In the days before the world began, Mu gave birth to the sun and taking Her sun as Her lover, She gave birth to the moon. Mating with her grandson Moon, She brought forth the stars, so many that they filled the heavens. Then mating with the stars, the sacred womb of Mu once again stirred with life so that in this way She brought forth all the animals and plants. It is for this reason that Cuna people remember that Mu Olokukurtilisop gave birth to the universe—created all that exists.

The first Cuna people made their homes in the caves of Tarcarcuna but even when they wandered as far as the Chucunaque River, still they brought their dead back to the caves of the mountain, there to rest in the womb of Mother Mu, the protective womb from whence all people came.

Close to the caves of Tarcarcuna, stands the sacred group of saptur, trees whose fruit contains the juice of the menstrual blood of Mu. And close to the grove is the sacred hut of the Inna, the shrine of female puberty that each young woman enters at the time of her new womanhood, the time she celebrates the ceremonies of the Inna. On the ground near the Inna shrine, the young one lies being as one with the earth, as the older women toss the sacred soil upon her. Gathering in a circle about her, they sit on the benches to form the Ring of Protection, smoke rising from their pipes as incense invoking the spirit of Mu. Then removing the covering of earth, the women take the young one and paint the red juice of the saptur, the menstrual blood of Mu, upon her face—chanting their blessing on her life, honoring her with the dance of new womanhood.

Into the sacred Inna shrine, the young woman is escorted and there the black ribbons of her hair fall upon the earth, as her childhood falls from her in the woman shrine that no man has ever entered, the holy place of Mother Mu. Emerging from the Inna shrine as a full-grown woman, her golden brown face glowing with red saptur is now framed within her small black satin cap of woman hair—as she awaits the time of the omens.

One sacred saptur tree is felled by the women as a gift of Mu to the initiate. Carefully studying the cross-grain of the tree, the women read each and every line, foretelling the events of the new woman's life. Only now that the woman blood has begun to flow, only now that she is one with the earth, only now that the menstrual blood of Mu has brightened her face, only now that her head is free from the weight of the hair of her childhood—is the young woman dedicated to the Goddess Mu Olokukurtilisop, brought into the sacred fold of womanhood and provided with her secret Cuna name that she will tell no others to the end of her days on earth.

Hsi Ho

These scanty references to the Goddess as Hsi Ho appear in the *Shan Hai Ching* and the *Huai Nan Tzu,* both texts of the Han period. In these writings, Hsi Ho is said to live beyond the southeastern waters, in an area referred to as the Sweet Waters, *Kan Shui.* Even more minimal remnants of information about the nature of Hsi Ho appear in the earlier Chou texts. The Fu Sang tree is generally thought to be a mulberry. Three hundred *li* is about one hundred miles. It may be completely coincidental, but it is interesting to realize that the concept of there being ten suns also appears in the beliefs of the Native American tribes of California.

Mother of the ten suns,
She who creates the heavenly bodies,
She who creates the calendar
of the ten days of the week—
She causes all to happen
by Her celestial design.

Each morning we may look upon
the Valley of Light,
watching Her bathe one of the suns,
the one that She has chosen for that day,
in the sweet waters of the Kan Yuan Gulf
and then watch Her place the sun
in the branches of the Fu Sang Tree
where it sits among the multitude of tiny leaves,
raised three hundred li into the sky,
until it starts upon its way
across the wide heavens

finally coming to rest
on western Yen Tzu Mountain,
only to return to Her again—
as each of us shall do
after our journey upon the earth.

Ala

Though the information that I was able to find on the Goddess
of the Ibo people of Nigeria is scanty, it does reveal several major
attributes of the nature of Her importance. Ala is both the provider
of life and the Mother who receives again in death, both attributes
revealing Her high position among the people who revere Her.
It is also Ala who proclaims the law that is the basis for all moral
human behavior. In this last attribute, we may see a concept of
the Goddess such as that found in the images of Demeter and
Isis as providers of the law, or perhaps the understanding that the
Mother of all explains the law through Her works, a theological
concept close to that found in China. Most interesting is the custom
of having life-size images of Ala sitting on the porch of a small
wooden house in the village, visible to all who pass by. This custom
may well be one that grew from the worship of the Goddess as
ancestress or grandmother, Her image and spirit still dwelling in
the village.

Holy Mother Earth,
She who guides those who live upon Her,
She whose laws the people of the Ibo follow,
living in the honesty and rightness
that are the ways of Goddess Ala;
it is She who brings the child to the womb
and She who gives it life,
always present during life
and receiving those whose lives are ended,
taking them back into Her sacred womb,
"the Pocket of Ala"

Along the Benue River
where the waters slide into the mighty Niger
and through its many fingers,
flow into the sea,
the women and the men
join in building the Mbari,
sacred houses where Goddess Ala
child upon Her knee,
sword sometimes in Her hand,

looking out upon the Ibo world
as the Ibo look upon Her—
glad that She dwells close by.

Androcratic Thinking

Considering the formidable and consistent material available to us
on the Goddess, it is curious that She is surrounded with such an
unholy silence. It seems hard to imagine that She was unintentionally
overlooked. There are three main causes for Her being silenced: archaeological bias, linguistic bias, and traditional religious bias.

First, consider the artwork of circa 32,000–26,000 B.C. John Onians
puzzled over the meaning of the abundance of female representations
found there. To him, these images do not invite "ethnological comparisons" or "comparisons with totemism, shamanism, sympathetic magic,
or initiation rites." His only explanation was sexual. Considering the
Venus of Willendorf (circa 21,000 B.C.), he explains:

> those areas of her body which are shown in all their rounded perfection
> are precisely those which would be most important in the preliminary
> phases of lovemaking, that is, the belly, buttocks, thighs, breast and shoul-
> ders, while the lower legs, lower arms, feet and hands are withered to
> nothing. There is no real parallel for this enormous imbalance of attention
> in any later art. Equally without parallel is the total neglect of the face
> . . . This could once again relate to the restriction of interest during
> lovemaking, or more specifically the restriction to manual love play. This
> explains why the woman is so important in art.

This hypothesis is understandable—particularly for men—considering
the strong Freudian influence of this century. But it is just as likely
that a man did not create the sculpture in the first place, and even
if he did so, how can we assume this represents his erotic experience?

Is it conceivable that this artwork expresses not merely erotic
but symbolic or philosophic images? Marija Gimbutas supports this
alternative:

> Early artwork was thoroughly symbolic, inspired by the urge to create
> another world, the mythic world. We do not know when [the hu]man
> became the creator of myth, but certainly not as late as 30,000 years
> ago. The manifestation or belief in an afterlife and magical ceremonies
> is traced back to [the] Neanderthal [hu]man some 50,000 years ago.
> Ethnological evidence has shown that art is never dissociated from religious
> and social life. The same is true throughout prehistoric times and most
> of the historic era.

Of particular concern to Onians was the representation of vulvas, breasts, and large buttocks, about which Gimbutas observes: "Emphasized vulvas are not just 'female signs' (the term used by Leroi Gourhan), but are symbolic vulvas or wombs of the Goddess." Additionally Gimbutas asserts that

> the association of vulva and plant is as early as the upper palaeolithic [*sic*] art as was already demonstrated by Marshack in 1972. He rightly considered the vulva as a 'nonsexual,' that is, nonerotic symbol representing stories of processes that include birth and death, menstruation, and time-factored cycles relating to nature.

The representation of breasts can easily be interpreted as nurturance; many sculptures depict a woman-animal nursing her young. The sacred body part of the Goddess depicted as "large egg-shaped buttocks" is common throughout the Neolithic, Chalcolithic, and Copper ages, and is associated with the beginnings of life itself and not lovemaking *per se*.[17] Humbling as it might be to accept, perhaps our ancestors were not as sexually "hung-up" as we are!

Second, the overwhelming majority of archaeologists, historians, and theologians have been men "raised in societies that embrace the male-oriented religions of Judaism or Christianity."[18] These religious norms affect both their consideration and interpretation of given data. This is subtly evidenced in the use of language as well. The Goddess tradition has been referred to as a "cult" instead of a "religion," implying to the modern ear something less than acceptability. "One never reads of 'the religion of Artemis' and 'the cult of Jesus'; it is always the other way around."[19] The female deity stories are considered "myth," which Webster's defines as a story of "ostensibly historical events having only an imaginary or unverifiable existence." *Religious* is defined as "relating or devoted to the divine or that which is held to be of ultimate importance." *Religious scripture* is "the sacred writings of a religion considered authoritative," while *theology* means "a rational interpretation of religious faith, practice, and experience dealing with God and his [*sic*] relation to the world." Given our linguistic bias, it is difficult for contemporary peoples of the West to take seriously the beliefs, symbols, and creation stories of ancient peoples when they are described as myth, cult, and *pagan* (meaning "heathen, an irreligious person, strange, uncivilized, an unconverted member of a people or nation that does not acknowledge the God of the Bible, heathenish, barbarous"[20]— even when these ancient writings on clay tablets or papyruses bear witness as the oldest religious stories of our species.

We find it equally difficult to "regard the beliefs of the tribes of Dahomey in Africa, the Toba of Argentina, or the Chinese of ancient Chi' province, as anything more than interesting mythology, or intellectual curiosities." That three of the worlds major religions—Judaism, Christianity, and Islam—are not considered heathen religions leaves us wondering to what extent this is due to their being in

> the small minority of faiths that revere no female deities with their beliefs, each having made overt efforts to suppress earlier Goddess reverence—and to wonder, if when so called primitive people of today are converted to Christianity their acceptance of the New Testament then classifies that scripture as mythology?[21]

Equally to the point, how would it affect you if your religious beliefs, measured against the socially accepted belief system, were referred to as cultic and pagan? The power of language, which feminists have been repeatedly told for decades is trivial, has a large impact on our perspective as well as our self-image. And inclusive langauge, to be truly liberating, requires more than simply adding *she*.

Third, religious scholarship has cast the Goddess tradition in a promiscuous light. There were sacred women of the Goddess—*qadishtu*, the "undefiled," "sanctified," or "holy" women—who made love to various men and both they and their children were honorably accepted into society. This sacred sexual custom was part of the worship of the Divine Ancestress known in

> Sumer, Babylon, Anatolia, Greece, Carthage, Sicily, Cryprus, and even in Canaan. . . . Yet [these] sexual customs . . . were nearly always described as "prostitution," the sacred women nearly always described as "temple prostitutes" or "ritual prostitutes." The use of the word *prostitute* as a translation for *qadishtu* not only negates the sanctity of that which was held sacred,[22]

but also distorts its very meaning.

> Academic authors wrote of the sexually active Goddess as "improper," "unbearably aggressive," or "embarrassingly void of morals," while male deities who raped or seduced legendary women or nymphs were described as "playful," or even admirably "virile."[23]

As we shall explore later with more detail, the "lack of morals" for the invaders included murder, legalized rape, kidnapping, and the barbarous violation of indigenous peoples and culture, done in the name and at the explicit will of a violent male god.[24] Why are the ancient times of the Goddess not recognized for their contributions to civilization—to medicine, government, agriculture, ceramics, textiles, written language, and more. There appears to be no room for praise but only for misinterpreation and condemnation. It can also be argued that religious scholarship in the West has traditionally represented the vested interests of its own Judeo-Christian tradition, ridiculing polytheism as unthinkable while praising monotheism as essential, and assuming that the Goddess is really fragmented pieces of independent and possibly antagonistic little goddesses. It has cast any religious tradition that is concerned with sexuality and fertility as pagan heathenism and any female symbolism as "immoral." It has battled to maintain order; any challenge to its authority is anathema. Only in recent decades has it taken women and women's issues seriously; previously it assumed that the subordinate status of women was correct. These attitudes encourage a "pervasive prophetic intolerance toward other religions. . . . [S]pawn[ing] religious intolerance and a climate in which destruction of peoples who practice other religions can be countenanced."[25]

Patriarchal Invasions of Matriarchy

There are some who assert that the lives of women in a culture that honors the feminine Divine are not necessarily better than those in other cultures.[26] This would not appear to be the case for those who lived in the era of the Great Goddess. The Goddess tradition developed within a matrilineal, matrifocal society. It has frequently been described as matriarchal. However, matriarchy has come to mean many things. To some, it is a society governed by women; to Marxists it represents an egalitarian society where production and power is shared equally by women and men; to others it refers to the worship of the Goddess regardless of political systems. Matriarchy can also be described as the differentiation between female and male kinds of power, female power being expressed as "nonpossessive, noncontrolling and organic ways that are harmonious with nature" and respective of "female things," with male power as its opposite. Patriarchy has been identified with domination and manipulation, matriarchy with connectedness and intuition, seeking "nonauthoritarian and nondestructive power relationships and attitudes." To satisfy the need to do away with any 'archy, matristic societies are characterized by "spontaneity, sensuality, and antiauthoritarianism"; they are "generally matrifocal and matrilineal." The tradition of the Great Goddess flourished in a matristic environment that was quite possibly governed by women as well, and was, in that sense, matriarchal. But the most significant meaning of matriarchy is "an idea about women in freedom," and, in the time of the Goddess tradition, "certainly women held greater power than they do now."[27]

Much of the early power of women was related to the miracle of their bodies. There was a great awe for women and women's mysteries: painless, cyclical bleeding; reproducing and birthing humans from their bodies; producing food from their bodies to feed the newly born. There was some awareness that lovemaking produced children. Carved some eight thousand years ago in Catal Hüyük, a relief depicts "the bodies of two lovers in a close embrace, (and on) the other side, a woman holding an infant."[28] However, since women were not confined to one mate, paternity could not be determined. Thus, all children were children of the mother; "the matrilineal clan was the bonding unit of matrifocal culture" developing religious myths and sacred practices to express the same human experience observed of the earth herself. "Earth is the bountiful female, the ever-giving Mother, Who sends forth food on Her surface in cyclical rhythms and receives our dead back into Her womb."[29] This gave women incredible power: power over their own bodies (which is still in great dispute today), power in their relationships, and central societal power as leaders of the clan. Matrilineal naming of the young exerted economic and political power. From mother to daughter, land and rights were passed from generation to generation.[30] The prepatriarchal Goddess tradition, through its imagery, ritual, and social system "told women that power, awesomeness, and centrality were theirs by nature, not by privilege or miracle; the female was primary."[31] It was exactly this power that patriarchy needed to overcome.

The Goddess tradition was attacked by successive and successful invasions by nomadic peoples:

> Aryans in India, Hittites and Mittani in the Fertile Crescent, Luwians in Anatolia, Kurgans in eastern Europe, Achaeans and later Dorians in Greece, as well as Semitic people called Hebrews, who came from the deserts of the south.[32]

They considered themselves superior peoples. Their gods were gods of battle, the leadership of their high priests was without question, and their warriors reflected their aggressive gods. Their sacred symbol was a storm god, depicted by volcanoes, lightning, blazing fire, and the blade. The supremacy of their gods and the authority of the priestly caste created an attitude of a religious crusade, invading, conquering, destroying, and ruling the indigenous peoples with each cultural and territorial assault. This "dominator/dominated" mentality introduced a previously unknown dualism into society. The conquering dominating warriors were victorious, ushering in the dualistic concept of light as good and dark as evil, perhaps reflecting their racial bias toward the darker conquered peoples. The beginnings of slavery (that is, one person being owned and subjugated by another, to be bought and sold at the owner's discretion) is closely identified with these armed attacks.[33] A major ideological distinction between the tradition of the warrior god and the Goddess tradition is that the invaders defined power as "power over,"—the power to take, the power of control—while the Goddess tradition honored power that gave life, "power with," power that acknowledged the natural rhythm of nature. The invaders apparently believed in "the organized slaughter of other human beings, along with the destruction and looting of their property and the subjugation and exploitation of their persons," as necessary, acceptable behavior and normative to their way of life. "The way they characteristically acquired material wealth was not by developing technologies of production, but through ever more effective technologies of destruction." And so it is to this day.

As men began to realize their part in procreation, they claimed greater and greater power for themselves. "Gradually male dominance, warfare, and the enslavement of women and of gentler, more 'effeminate' men became the norm." Massive cultural shifts ensued, and the survivors' task was to somehow integrate these disparate ideologies, creating what Gimbutas calls "hybrid cultures" where the worship of the Goddess became increasingly more dangerous yet somehow survived for hundreds of years, underground, in the hearts and psyches of the common, peasant people.[34]

In order to disassemble and gain control of the power structure of the Goddess tradition, swift, severe, and exacting laws had to be established restricting the sexual rights of women. The custom of the *qadishtu* had to be eliminated. To gain economic and political power, matrilineal naming had to be replaced with patrilineal naming. A whole ethical system had to be invented, a new morality, in order to assure male supremacy, because

> a woman who behaves as a sexually and economically free person *is* a threat to the entire social and economic fabric of a rigidly male-dominated society. Such behavior cannot be countenanced lest the entire social and economic system fall apart."[35]

We can trace the development of this new morality. Even as late as circa 2000 B.C., a man who raped a woman would be put to death.

This was true in Babylonia during the time of Hammurabi, even though some invasions had already taken place. However, circa 1450–1250 B.C., in the laws of Assyria, if a woman was raped, her father or husband was to rape the rapist's wife or daughter. The father could also require his daughter to marry the man who raped her. In Hebrew law, additionally, a raped woman, if married or betrothed, would be put to death. Assyrian law also enforced the death penalty for a woman who had an abortion.[36]

Patrilineal naming requires the oppression of women, allowing patriarchy to thrive. With the change in the matrilineal system, the economic status and even the potential for the economic independence of women was thwarted. Further laws were established to dictate what women may or may not inherit, until eventually women were treated as mere possessions of men, with no legal or moral recourse. A new morality had been invented, and through the enforcement of these new laws of God, the ancient sexual customs were denounced as depraved, pagan, and wicked. The Hebrew Levite priests "devised the concept of sexual 'morality': premarital virginity for *women*, marital fidelity for *women*, in other words total control over the knowledge of paternity."[37]

With this shifting of sexual norms, the economic and political power of women was shattered. The spiritual power of the Great Goddess, however, still reigned within. For patriarchy to succeed it would need to expropriate the images, symbols, and rituals of the Goddess tradition to meet its own needs. Some of the changes are subtle, others grotesque.

In the earliest periods there are the Sumerian transitions, from the most ancient Creator Goddess Nammu to the less powerful Inanna, the loss of power by the Goddess Ereshkigal, through the trickery and violence of the male deity Nergal. Kuan Yin, whose image may be derived from the pre-Buddhism Creator Goddess Nu Kwa, is described as having once been a male boddhisatva [sic], who decided to return to earth as Kuan Yin. The Arabian Goddess Attar, associated with the Semitic Ishtar and the Egyptian Hathor, is described in later South Arabian inscriptions as a male deity. The effects of early Judaism are noticeable in the accounts of the Goddess of the Semites as Asherah and Ashtart; Ashtart (Ashtoreth) used as a name of a demon in the Middle Ages, though the gender was also changed to male. Early Christians made the Goddess Bridget into a Catholic saint, but doused Her eternal flame at Kildare; while later Christians burned the holy books of the Mayans, but appropriated the Tepeyac shrine of the Goddess Coatlicue and dedicated it to the Virgin Mary as the Lady of Guadalupe. Long after Saint Patrick destroyed the sacred cairn of the Cailleach Bheur in County Covan, missionaries in Hawaii encouraged converts to defy the Goddess Pele, by throwing stones into the crater that was sacred to Her.[38]

The deformation of the Goddess appears as a steady ripple throughout history. Speaking from the Judeo-Christian tradition, and living in a culture greatly informed by this tradition, I will detail some of the more stunning images and symbol reversals.

First, the notion of God calling a chosen people is common to both the Jewish and Christian belief systems. This automatically sets up a dualism of domination—the chosen versus the unchosen—requiring a covenantal agreement with a monotheistic deity and setting into motion the destruction (or at least negative judgment) of any outside group.[39] At the time of the inception of Judaism, the outsider was the Goddess tradition, influencing the worship and ritual of indigeous peoples. She had to be destroyed. The same scenario, in somewhat different shades, happened in early Christianity, and in vast missionary efforts worldwide and throughout its history.

Second, the sacred writings of the chosen people had to eliminate as much as possible the presence of the Goddess. This elimination caused great difficulty for the early Canaanites who worshiped the Goddess Ashtoreth—also referred to as Asherah, Astarte, Attoret, Anath, Elat, or Baalat—as their chief divinity. As the Hebrew people settled in that area, they tried continually to undermine Her powerful presence. The Levite priests joined Her with Baal, "mispronounced her name (reciting it as *boseth,* meaning "shame"), and, referring to Her only in the masculine gender, refused to even recognize the position of the Goddess."[40] The intention of the people of Yahweh was to destroy the existing culture through the desecration of Goddess shrines and sanctuaries, massacres, and, as witnessed most vividly in the Bible, merciless as well as cowardly treatment of women."[41]

Nonetheless, there are frequent citings in Scripture of the people worshiping the ancient Goddess Ashtoreth/Asherah,[42] whose presence was found everywhere—on hills, under trees, next to altars—represented as a pole, a statue, and most powerfully as a living tree. These tree representations were called *asherah,* and although not explicitly connected to references of the Goddess Asherah, a connection seems obvious. It is likely that the *asherim* (plural) were fig trees, called sycamore figs, considered to be the "Body of the Goddess on Earth." She is known from Egyptian writings and murals as the Goddess Hathor, also called the Lady of the Sycamore and Serpent Lady, for "to eat of its fruit was to eat of the flesh and fluid of the Goddess." Other murals actually decpit the Goddess *within* the tree, "passing out its sacred fruit to the dead as the food of eternity, immortality and continued life, even after death." Other references to the Goddess symbolized as the tree are also found in Crete and India, as well as in the Isis/Osiris story. One may recall Ezekiel reprimanding the people as "idolators" who passed the sacred branch, as well as the occasion when Jesus is said to have cursed the fig tree.[43] As Mary Daly has pointed out, our Christmas celebrations include cutting down a tree so that a male savior can be born.[44] As discussed earlier, the serpent was also a great symbol of the Goddess, honored as the source of wisdom and prophetic counsel, who in Sumer was called Great Mother Serpent of Heaven. The cobra preceded the name of the Goddess Herself in the ancient Egyptian Goddess tradition and became the hieroglyphic sign for the word *Goddess*.[45]

These two powerful Goddess symbols are intentionally expropriated and redefined in the Genesis story as the final blow to convince us forever that the Goddess was our downfall. In the Goddess tradition women and men were created together but in the religion of the male god, "it was of ultimate importance that the male was made first, and in the image of his creator." Despite the Levites' knowledge of actual birth, they insist that the female is born from the male, echoing a similar misappropriation of birthing in the Greek story of Athena being born from the head of Zeus. The serpent tempting Eve to disobey God's command, the tree of forbidden fruit offering knowledge of good and evil in the guise of sexual consciousness—these symbols have been negatively redefined to remind us that whatever is associated with the Goddess is dangerously pagan and sinful. Furthermore, we are told that it is the will of God that Eve desire only her husband, giving divine sanction to the patrilineal system. Gradually we begin to realize that "the events of the Paradise myth, one by one, betray the political intentions of those who first invented the myth."[46]

In order to assure male supremacy, power to control the family incorporated both political and spiritual power. As is true in Greek mythology as well,

> men would have to pit the *concept* of Fatherhood against the *fact* of Motherhood. . . . Through a violent and unnatural act of will, Fathers, not Mothers, would be the starting point of culture and knowledge. . . . [So that men could] experience themselves as divine.[47]

In Greek mythology, the power of the Goddess, and therefore the power of women, had to be split in order to become manageable: the "good" mother could be retained only at the expense of the "bad" mother. Nurturance was acceptable, especially the nurturing of children and/or men. However, female sexual autonomy and/or economic independence had to be terminated. Placing women in either-or roles is essential to patriarchy, not only to undermine the power of the woman herself, but because "a fully realized female tends to engender anxiety in the insecure male. Unable to cope with a multiplicity of powers united in one female," the Greeks splintered female power into rivaling goddesses, archetypal images as envisioned by males; otherwise, a female equivalent to Zeus could reemerge.

Particularly threatening was women's sexual power. On the one hand, therefore, a virgin goddess's asexuality freed men to relate to her without intimidation, as in the goddess Athena. On the other hand, rape myths portray the seduction of a virgin and bring her under male control, as in the case of Persephone. Some see these myths as an animus-integration effort, reporting that even today women may frequently fantasize being overpowered by a man and forced to submit. However, these fantasies are a form of masochism, and, as suggested by Karen Horney, "are the result of women's repression by society." Violence is always an insult to women's integrity and innate power.[48]

One way or another, the Greek myths destroyed the Goddess image and portrayed women as broken pieces of a once-whole cloth.

> The great Hera was made into a disagreeable, jealous wife; Athena was made into a cold, masculine daughter; Aphrodite was made into a frivolous sexual creature; Artemis was made into the quite forgettable sister of Apollo; and Pandora was made into the troublesome, treacherous source of human woes. These prototypes later evolved into the wicked witch, the cruel stepmother, the passive princess, etc., of our fairy tales.[49]

The Bloody Sacrifice

The most profound symbol of the Goddess and the power of womanhood is blood. Symbolically, blood is birthing/dying power, a natural process of creativity and of letting go. There is no need for human or animal sacrifice or expiation for sins. The earliest blood experience was woman's blood and it was totally natural as a cosmic and personal experience. Deformed and expropriated by patriarchy, blood is now experienced directly by women and indirectly by men with mixtures of fear, disgust, and a strong need for an antiseptic.

In several later mythological accounts, we have access to the legend of the sacred marriage *(hieros gamos),* symbolized by the marriage of the High Priestess (the Goddess) and her consort, a young male who was referred to both as son and as husband. After the marriage, he became king, having achieved access to the divine through his relationship to the queen. He held this privileged position for the duration of his reign, probably one year, which terminated, it is generally believed, in his violent death. The myths then depict the Goddess mourning the death of her lover. The blood sacrifice of the youth is accorded meaning as a fertility ritual related to the natural birth/death earth processes which women's menstrual flow originally symbolized. Over time, substitutes—effigies and animal sacrifices—came into play. There is evidence that around 1200 B.C. "the year" was extended to the duration of the king's virility and health. However, in one of the earliest legends, that of the Sumerian Goddess Inanna (written around 2000 B.C. though likely to have originated considerably earlier, before the written word), the consort king's death was the result not of a fertility ritual but of an act of disobedience. Once he no longer lived in accordance with the laws of the Goddess, he would be sacrificed. And the Goddess would weep and mourn his death, although She Herself ordered his demise. This perhaps marks the shift from nonsacrifical natural menstrual blood to sacrifical male blood. Thus it can be suggested that when we live our lives in accordance with natural law, we prosper. But when we betray that law, putting ourselves above it and pretending to have power over it, we are destroyed. Today we might interpret this as the human lack of ecological respect for the earth. And the result of such continued arrogance will also be death.

While the death of the male sometimes was averted through substitutes, other practices also developed, including the shedding of blood through castration and circumcision. Perhaps the origin of the Freudian fear of being castrated by women, voluntary castration was a way the young consort could in fact save his life while assuring his faithfulness to the Goddess. Perhaps it was by identifying themselves so closely with the Goddess, by ridding themselves of their maleness and wearing women's clothing, that men gradually gained entrance into the priesthood of the Goddess, slowly replacing the priestesses. Removing women from their religious functions limits their overall status. The invaders and conquerors certainly would not abide ritual regicide or the political and spiritual power of the high priestess.[50] So their expropriation of blood-letting power took the form of circumcision, with a "magic blood" claimed through male puberty rites. For the Hebrews, this rite/right became the dictate of a male god, signifying the privilege and command of the chosen people, whose law was not the natural cycle of life and death but political invasion and domination. When there is no recognition of women's natural blood power, it becomes disfigured and projected onto an enemy, and blood will indeed be shed.

Rituals involving blood, particularly the consumption of blood, are powerful spiritual/psychic transformative images. There is an ancient

Hindu Tantric ritual dedicated to the female savior Charis that later developed into a Gnostic rite. In this ceremony, a cup of wine is miraculously turned into Charis's blood so that Her grace can flow through all. The women present, representing Charis "in person and in presence" would consecrate "the cup with an effusion of Charis proceeding from themselves."[51] In *The Natural Genesis,* Gerald Massey asserts that it is this ritual that is the basis for today's Christian liturgy.

> The blood of Charis preceded the blood of Christ, and there would have been no doctrine of cleansing by the blood of Christ but for the purification by the blood of Charis. The male Messiah or word of God would have not come arrayed in the garment dipped in blood, if blood had not been the feminine manifestor of the Word as Wisdom.

Massey further asserts that "the change of the sex did but turn the typical mystery into meaningless mystification."[52] Whereas male assimilation of female mysteries can create greater consciousness for the male, suppression of the natural mystical female experience creates an unholy and unnatural dualistic barrier between inner and outer, from which we all greatly suffer.[53] Thus, while early Christians ultimately interpreted the bloody sacrifice of Jesus of Nazareth as an expiation for sins (now needed because of our break with natural law?), their failure to recognize its essential femaleness rendered women impotent and left them subjugated under male jurisdiction and a distorted symbol system.

Over time women were disengaged and disempowered as essential to sacred ritual and personal-communal transformation. Nonetheless, women still continue to bleed, and, as such, have blood power by natural inheritance. This power, however, has been broken in two in order to be more easily controlled. The fracture within women's psyche can be understood in light of society's view regarding menstruation. This view, to a great extent, has been so damaging to women's self-understanding that it is not an exaggeration to say that women have been pscyhologically castrated, as well as, as in many cultures, sexually mutilated.[54] Out of touch with the creative wholeness of women's blood power, this split depicts women as "the good little ovulating mother and the fiend of menstruation." Ovulation, because it represents women's capacity to bear children, which is how women are generally perceived in this culture, is considered a positive contribution to society. Menstruation, on the other hand, is regarded negatively: it is "seen as merely an excretory process: a simple stripping-off of the walls of the womb because the 'disappointed egg' has not been fertilized."[55] When a woman bleeds, she is unclean, sick, odd, self-conscious, strangly empowered.

Women's blood power—and male abuse of that power—can be portrayed as two women from Christian Scripture: "Mary Magdalene, the prostitute: the woman who had sex without having a child; and Mary Virgin: the woman who had a child without having sex."[56] There is, however, another possibility: this unacceptable dark side of a woman, the menstrual aspect of a natural cycle, can stimulate within her an inner centeredness that simultaneously engenders independence and cosmic connection. A woman can at this time develop her virgin qualities: becoming a woman unto herself, in touch with Self and with instinctive renewing powers; intricately and intimately meshed with a dark enveloping universe. Women may, responding to their own inner rhythm, seek time alone in silence for secluded meditation. In many cultures such "time alone" customs have been sabotaged and become cruel practices requiring women to remove themselves from men—not for meditation, but because men have deemed bleeding women dangerous.

Women's wise wound has profound effects upon men. Because of ovulation, men can become the fathers of children—in a patrilineal system, a movement toward power and immortality. During menstruation, however, women embody powers beyond their control, while remaining sexually appealing. Georg Groddeck considers menstruation exceedingly powerful for three rasons. First, sexual intercourse is highly desirable at this time. Second, deep childhood experiences are related to menstruating mothers. Our earliest sensory memories as infants are associated with women's bodies while bleeding. Our very act of birth is a blood-experience. Blood, as an archaic olfactory stimulus, embodies primitive dangers and energies. Third, bleedings "arouse the fear that we ourselves [men] can be made into women."[57] It is likely that the mother's personal integration is reflected in the mother/child relationship, greatly influencing the positive or negative directions of intense energies. If she is affirming of her own femaleness relative to the involvment of the father, she will pass on positive female dispositions and a balanced nurturance to both her daughters and her sons. If not, she will continue to perpetuate negativity to both as well. Since there is continued intense cultural-religious bias against women (even though in recent decades women have received support in their struggle toward personal integration), this negativity is still likely.

The Holocaust

Women's blood power, the central focus of all of women's powers and mysteries, has had an incredible influence over men's attitudes and behavior, "arousing at once his own instinct and his dread of its power. . . . [Making] him aware of his helplessness in face of his own instinctive desire."[58] Unresolved fear leads to hatred and violence. This violence was fully expressed during what is known as the Renaissance— generally understood as a time of discovery and enlightenment, a time of reevaluation and reformation. For women, it was a torturously different story.

Witchhunts—involving the arrest, torture, and ultimate execution of millions of peasant women—were sanctioned in a papal bull by Pope Innocent VIII in 1484. The Inquisition, which had directed itself to the mass murder of "heretics," now focused its torments on women it considered witches.

> The devil, in the mind of the witchhunters, was an actual being, and Witches were charged with having actual social and sexual intercourse with him. They were accused of . . . . [N]ight flights, turning people into animals, and charming away penises and hiding them in birds' nests.[59]

Women and witchcraft became associated with insatiable carnal lust, wicked sexuality, sin. Tertullian, as early as 22 A.D., had called women "the gate of hell." Now women's secret pact with the devil was considered signed in blood, understood as menstrual blood.[60] In *Malleus Malefircarum*, written by two Dominican inquisitors, Kramer and Sprenger, in 1486, witchcraft was considered a "special crime to which the ordinary laws of evidence did not apply," dictating the execution of nine million or more witches—mostly women—for two and a half centuries.[61] The "laws of evidence" allowed execution for hideous crimes confessed under torture.

> Sometimes torture went on for days and nights, as in Germany, and sometimes it was limited to an hour at a time, as in Italy and Spain. So-called torture was banned altogether in England, where starvation, deprivation of sleep, and gang-rape did not count as torture.[62]

The persecution of witches was not an isolated political maneuver on the part of the ecclesiastical authorities. It was part of a wider political and economic attack on society involving the expropriation of natural resources and land; the establishment of professional elitist groups; and the establishment of a "work ethic" value system supported by a transcendent God. In each case, women were prime targets.

Feudal society granted privilege to the few while requiring that small parcels of land be available to the peasants for their own use, keeping them on the edge of poverty. Nonetheless, their small piece of land was their hope. With the practice of private property, families lost their land and became totally dependent on their employer, sinking deeper into poverty. This was most destructive for women, who were largely responsible for the care of children. While men could go off and work in a nearby town, women remained home. "Women's work" was devalued as no longer central to the life of the community. Peasant villages were no longer economically viable, and hence no longer socially viable. Feasts and folk celebrations, mingled with a pagan pseudo-Christianity, were outlawed by the church. These changes in land rights ushered in an age which "saw nature as nonalive and as something valuable only when it could be exploited." This kind of massive exploitation bears the earmarks of the ecological debt we have inherited to this day.

Another major political and economic move was the expropriation of knowledge. Services previously provided by local people were suddenly "professionalized" by a male-defined group of experts who were paid for their services. This required specific education, certified only by those expert professionals. And this education was "to be sold only to those who could afford to buy it." Clearly, women, until quite recently, need not apply. Women were in fact forbidden to get the education deemed necessary for them to do their work. If they dared to work without official church approval, they were labeled as witches and as such must die. A prime example is in the area of healing. For centuries, women were involved in natural healing processes and midwifery. Now, as witches, as evil creatures, they were forbidden such practice. The effect on the patient is equally noticeable, especially among the poor. "If I am forced to give power-over my own being to someone who represents an elite from which my kind are excluded, my confidence in myself, in my own ability and right to control my own destiny is weakened."[63] Women, particularly poor "uneducated" women, echo the same words today.

Lastly, with the emphasis on a transcendent God outside of creation, land could more easily be exploited. The peasants, who were still in touch with the land as sacred, were no longer able to till the soil. Work, and the money earned, became a transcedent life value. Work was defined "as the only true purpose of this life." And as women became increasingly "excluded from productive labor," they were "forced into the role of object." Wealthy women could enjoy the status of their husbands, a vicarious living style enjoyed by many women today. But for a woman to be her own person would be too threatening. Poor women were designated as hopeless. Women, devaluing themselves, not trusting their own inner experience, frequently viewed each other with suspicion and distrust. "To both sexes, the role of victim was made to seem the woman's natural and deserved role." To accept the victimization of women is to accept the victimization of all matter—sensuality, sexuality, earth, darkness, birthing, Divine Immanence.[64] Dualism run rampant!

Women's mysteries are connected to the Moon Goddess. One of the representations of the threefold nature of the Moon Goddess is a primitive swastika.[65] Struck by both the Goddess symbolism and this century's political use of the swastika, I was curious to discover the connection between two holocausts, separated by centuries, yet both symbolically represented by a swastika. What is the connection between the massacre of women and the massacre of Jews? Rosemary Ruether, in her book *New Woman, New Earth,* comments that during the Inquisition, both Jews and women were treated with contempt:

> The Jew was seen as a devil worshiper, equipped with horns, claws, and tail, riding on a satanic goat. Like the Witch, the Jew was believed to steal the Eucharist and to perform other blasphemous caricatures of Catholic rituals.[66]

The Jewish tradition honors the celebration of the Goddess of the Sabbath, connected to the festival celebration of the full moon. Originally, "the feast of the full moon called the *shabattu* was the feast *which celebrated the menstruation of the great Goddess.*" The connection between these two holocausts is women's blood mysteries, associating Jews with vestiges of their ancient Goddess worship, practiced as sexual union.[67]

In order to gain political support for mass murder, one must project one's enemies as evil, characterizing them as the embodiment of all undesirable traits. During the Middle Ages, women were the scapegoats of the church, persecuted to eliminate women's power and invent a new economic order. Heretics and Jews were persecuted as well. Any person seen as a threat by the patriarchal system had to be eliminated, by whatever means. "Among ancient propaganda against Jews is the charge that the men, as well as the women, menstruate," and fear of menstrual blood was paramount to the witchhunters. As with the women of the Witch-burning holocaust, so too the Jews of the Nazi holocaust, which claimed to purge society of undesirables, "gave the illusion that the community was now improved. . . . The common enemy united the persecutors."[68]

Women Bonding: The Experience of Wicca

Despite millennia of persecution, the Goddess lives. Indeed, there is a reawakening of the Goddess, gathering women and men together to celebrate Her presence and Her power. This is called the Old Religion, sometimes referred to as Witchcraft, Wicca, the Craft, or perhaps in its broadest terms, Paganism. As a religion its intent is to make conscious the Divine-Human connection in relationship to the cosmos. The way it achieves this goal is through its craft: techniques to bring about practical results for personal and communal healing and growth. It is nonhierarchal, operating in small groups or covens that strive to assist each member to be in touch with her or his creative energies.[69] The members are "witches," a word that brings discomfort to most of us outside the craft. This discomfort is largely a remnant of fear caused by the false propaganda disseminated about women and their power during the Witch-burnings persecutions. A Witch is simply one who has been initiated into the coven after a long training period. The leadership moves among the group cultivating each member as a priestess, priest, or shaman. Leadership "cannot be assumed, inherited, appointed, or taken for granted, and it does not confer the right to control another."[70]

The Goddess gatherings focus on the power of experience, of connecting with the Goddess Within who gives birth to an awakened, empowered personal and communal response. The Goddess is immanent— present in all life forms—in nature, in relationships, in communities. She is *here,* as unconditional presence and power. To experience the immanence of the Goddess is to become increasingly aware "of the world and everything in it as alive, dynamic, interdependent, interacting, and infused with moving energies: a living being, a weaving dance." The Goddess is female because She gives life, and values creation as Her own body. This female image is inclusive of men because, as Mother, She gives birth to the male as well as to the female.[71]

The Goddess is known in Her three aspects, the Original Blessed Trinity. Even the Greeks, who celebrated powerful male deities, experienced their goddesses as female trinities.[72] The trinitarian aspects of the Goddess, unlike the Christian Trinity, include darkness as well as light, death as well as life. "To the ancients her contradictory character was an essential factor, frankly recognized."[73] This is unthinkable from the Christian perspective, which projects God as good and the devil as evil. The Moon Goddess, waxing in fullness and waning, portrays the cyclical nature of life. First She grows and develops, then dies. The cultural resistance to this *fact of life* refuses to admit the inner movement we all experience: the Goddess is both womb and tomb. She is not evil, nor our enemy. Rather, She embodies the truth: there is no life without death without life without death without life without . . . To try to overcome this natural life/death fact is to pretend to an ego consciousness and immortality that is both naïve and unreal.

The three aspects of the Moon Goddess are a reflection of our lives. As the waxing moon, the Virgin Goddess as woman unto herself is "the fresh light of dawn that sweep away weariness with the promise of new beginnings," awakening an inner wildness to be young, free, alive, and even outrageous—to be yourself, make your own choices, find your own power. As full moon, the Mother Goddess is fully embodied, passionate, and powerful. "She is Ripeness," birther, nourisher, teacher, and disciplinarian. The male is both Her husband and Her child. She is wildly and violently protective of those She loves. Yet She is neither blind nor sentimental; She exercises an unrelenting standard of viability over her young. As waning moon, She becomes the Wisdom Goddess typically represented as the Crone, the Hag, the Old Woman. She is the gateway to death, the slow decay and surrendering of life we each must experience. However, within Her great powers are the powers of renewal, connecting Her back once again to the Virgin, to rebirth, to the possibilities of newness.[74] Just as there is new seed in the withered flower, the Crone gives birth to the Virgin. The Crone is the most powerful of the three persons in as much as death is our greatest fear and perhaps greatest hope. The Crone in the Goddess tradition is the priestess for the final rites of passage, containing within herself Wisdom. This Original, Holy, Blessed Trinity is known then, as Creator, Preserver, and Destroyer. Personified as Kali, for example, "She was both ugly and beautiful, Virgin and Crone, darkness and light, winter and summer, birth giver and death bringer." The early Oriental Goddess worshipers recognized a truth: there is "constant simultaneous creation and destruction. . . . [E]very form is temporary, running through its own cycle from burgeoning growth to decline, death, and decay." Life is eternally cyclical. The Crone, welcoming us back into the virgin tomb of Mother Earth becomes the dark womb of regeneration.[75] In the Christian effort to deny the Crone as decaying matter is an effort to deny death as the birthing place of new life coming from the earth. Christianity envisioned renewed life as separate from the earth, as residing in heaven, which is essentially for souls only, an antimaterial blissful infinity of worship for a Transcendent Being equally disconnected from matter, earth, and creation. Here the truth of this Goddess-Crone becomes all the more threatening.

The celebrations of the Goddess religion follow the natural cycle of the earth and cosmic realities. Small groups of witches gather in covens to celebrate eight feasts, or sabbats, representing the solar theme and the natural fertility theme. The lesser sabbats are equinox and solstice celebrations. The greater sabbats are Imbolg, also called Candlemas, February 2; Bealtaine, also known as May Eve, April 30; Lughnasadh, or Lady Day Eve, July 31; and Samhain, which is still commonly celebrated as All Hallows Eve, October 31. There are several "schools of thought" that influence the style of celebration for these feasts: Gardnerian, Alexandrian, Traditional, Celtic, Dianic, and Saxon, to name a few. The Alexandrian and Gardnerian lines try to work with female and male partners so as to balance the psychic input. Even so, the emphasis on the Goddess's gift of intuition is considered the source of the God's gift of logic. Nonetheless, some covens, depending on their needs, are composed of women only. Janet and Stewart Farrar strongly support the development of both Goddess and God psychic energies, asserting that the next evolutionary task "is to revive the gift of the Goddess at full strength and *combine the two*—with unimaginable prospects for the human race and the planet we live on. . . . [Requiring] a special emphasis *on that which is to be reawakened*," specifically, the Goddess.[76]

At the completion of a long training period, the initiate is welcomed ceremoniously into the coven. Starhawk recommends daily disciplines for all coven members: regular physical exercise, daily meditation or visualization, keeping a magical diary called the Book of Shadows (a sort of personal journal). There are certain qualities or energies evoked during coven gatherings that facilitate their magic. The language of magic is expressed through spells, a cone of power, and trances. "A spell is a symbolic act done in an altered state of consciousness, in order to cause a desired change." Casting a spell projects into a symbol the energy needed for the spell. This projection requires an expansion of consciousness, or "a deliberate self-identification with other objects and people." Thus, the witch must develop a strong will through self-honesty, self-discipline, commitment, and conviction. The energy needed flows in spirals, called the cone of power, beginning and ending in a natural flow. To honor this natural flow, it is essential to begin and end the magic grounded, understood as connected to the earth's energy from which our life and energy flow. A trance is the overall shift or expansion of awareness that directs the magic. A trance expands perception beyond physical boundaries, leaving us open to energies helpful for healing and creativity. A trance can be induced through relaxation techniques, sensory isolation, rhythmic sounds, or boredom. Since the energy released is powerful, caution must be observed. (Beyond trances, of course, expanded consciousness can be facilitated by working with dreams.[77])

Wicca celebrates the unconditional love of the Goddess. She does not require bloody sacrifice or the sacrifice of our needs or desires. This is particularly helpful to women, who can begin to see themselves as worthy of celebration. Life naturally requires dyings and sacrifices—we need not devise our own. Discipline, courage, and empowerment are encouraged over asceticism, self-abnegation, and surrender. Men find liberation through the Horned God, who represents His own life/death polarity through tenderness and power. As the hunter, He is the Dying God always in union with greater life forces. His sexuality is a fully embodied, holy, connecting power. "He is the power of feeling," and the image of "the undivided Self in which mind is not split from body, nor spirit from flesh." This is a liberating image for men who have suffered in our patriarchal culture. For men to relate to the experience of Wicca, however, they must give up the traditional understanding of male power as well as traditional religious concepts. There is no all-knowing father-god to turn to and no social or religious system to support superiority. Men of the craft are challenged to "interact with strong, empowered women who do not pretend to be anything less than what they are."[78] Indeed, as more women and men continue to struggle to greater self-understanding, the challenge for each of us is to be who we are.

Perhaps the greatest challenge to women is to trust our own inner truth, to trust ourselves and not to be afraid to claim our power. And to know we are not alone. As we continue to bond together, we honor our past while envisioning our future and offer courage and hope for all the life forms that call this planet home. Embraced by the aweful power of the Goddess, we dare to bring forth new life once again:

> As if in slow motion, the fibers of rooted life-systems uplifted, pulled at each other, agonizingly deliberate. Earth smells mingled with each break-age, the ground in constant tremor. The air awaited in silent anticipation. Creaking shivers widened into a cosmic cry! Slowly, deliberately, know-ingly, all was ripped asunder. The ground swell released a final laborious push. Goddess emerged. Birthed, though still in peril, She endures, abiding amidst the rubble caused by Her very presence.
>
> This earthquake, erupting and collapsing the accepted mode of behavior called Western civilization, has stirred unconsciously for many centuries. Now She is reborn in our age, as the central focused energy, the "from everlasting," pleading, exhorting, demanding. To choose Her is to choose interdependence, nurturance, vulnerability, balance, integrity, compassion. To choose Her is to choose mystery and deep silent wisdom. To deny,

delay, marginalize, or hold Her in quiet contempt, is to choose death.

There is both urgency and steadfastness in Her eyes. She is in hard labor, straining, pushing, moaning, striving, to birth compassion in us. She is steadfast, convicted, firmly resolved. "If you would live," She announces, "you—all of you—must accept Me! And not just accept me passively, but embrace, cherish, strengthen, affirm, proclaim! I, the Ancient Earth-Mother, the Unconscious Lover, the Absolute Dark Trust, the Creative Empowering Presence that you have refused to acknowledge, I am Goddess. Behold! I make all things new!"

Chapter Four

The Christian Trinity
and the Feminine Divine

For the first time in recorded history, women in significant numbers are speaking from and writing of their experiences of the Divinity. Those of the Christian tradition who choose to remain within it often find that their experiences do not fit easily into the great teachings of that tradition. Sometimes, when one searches into the "nooks and crannies," the tradition will yield evidence that resonates with one's religious experience. Such was the case when, in chapter 1, we presented images of the Holy Spirit as the feminine Divine. In that chapter, among other issues, we looked at the feminine Holy Spirit within the context of the trinitarian relationship.

In this chapter, we will continue to explore the relationship of the feminine Divine and the Christian Trinity. We will do so through the presentation of two theological models. In the first model, each trinitarian Person will be seen as reflecting both a feminine and a masculine dimension. In the second model, each trinitarian Person will be described in gender-neutral language. In addition, we will discuss some of the trinitarian issues that are problematic in regard to a harmonious joining of the doctrine of the Trinity and the experience of the Divinity as feminine. These issues are the *filioque* clause (designating, in the creeds, the procession of the Spirit from the Son in addition to its procession from the Father), and the use of the word *Abba* as exemplifying Jesus' religious experience of the Divinity.

Androgyny

The idea that the human—or divine—person is not simply male or female, but rather contains both, is an idea as old as historical time itself. This idea is expressed by the word *androgyny,* which "can be

83

defined as the One which contains the Two; namely, the male *(andro-)* and the female *(gyne)*."[1] Androgyny refers not to that which is external but to that which exists within the individual.[2] Androgyny may be seen as the way to completeness. Androgynous thinking is found in such diverse sources as mythology, astrology, Greek philosophy, Gnosticism, alchemy, Cabalism, Taoism, Tibetan Tantrism, and Kundalini Yoga, as well as in the writings of Jung and in the experiences of contemporary people.[3]

To limit ourselves to only one tradition, that of polytheism, Judith Ochshorn would characterize both its gods and goddesses as androgynous. Thus, for example, as well as displaying traditionally "feminine" qualities, the goddesses were often self-defining and strong, even warlike, while the gods were concerned with such "feminine" functions as fertility and mercy, as well as with death.[4] Furthermore, sexuality in general, and female sexuality in particular, was seen as good. And the androgynous nature of the deities had a counterpart in cultic practices where women held positions of authority and power. Ochshorn contrasts this polytheistic society to those which are monotheistic, and specifically to Judeo-Christian monotheism as it is portrayed in the Scriptures. In the Judeo-Christian cultural context she finds a high degree of ambivalence toward the female, with female sexuality often characterized as specifically evil or ritually unclean. Further, with the triumph of monotheism over polytheism, the prominence of women in cultic practices likewise is severely curtailed, if not eliminated altogether. Ochshorn would argue for a correlation between the nature of the Divine and the real life experiences of women.[5]

As already noted by June Singer, it is not only such ancient traditions as polytheism that are androgynous; this concept is also to be found in contemporary literature and psychology.[6] However, in writing on the literary scene, Carolyn G. Heilbrun notes that contemporary women authors are not androgynous in their writings. Rather, their books may be classed as feminist. She would contend that feminism is a step on the way to androgyny because women must begin by discovering who they are; we must self-define. She notes, "Women have only recently learned to tell the truth, first to one another and then to themselves."[7]

For some contemporary theologians as well, this model of imaging God/ess according to the fullness of humanity offers what they would consider to be the richest and most powerful image available.[8] How they theologize out of this androgynous model will be treated in the next section.

Androgynous Models and Contemporary Theology

Traditionally the claim has been made that, while Christians use the terms *Father, Son, His, He, God,* when talking about the Divinity, it is understood that God transcends sexuality. However, some contemporary theologians would argue that the exclusive use of masculine (or feminine, if that were the case) language, contradicts the claim to transcend sexuality. In other words, *Father* means male, *he* means male, *God* means male. However, there is hesitancy on the part of many Christian and Jewish theologians to use gender-free terms because our Deity is considered to be a personal Ultimate and not an impersonal power. Coming to terms with anthropomorphism would seem to be the price that one pays for retaining images of the Deity that are personal.[9] But if one takes seriously the experience of androgyny, our images of God/ess could be presented in a way that would do justice to the teaching in Genesis that, in some real way, our being created female and male is the basis for our imaging of the Divine, while at the same time paying honor to the fact that the fullness of humanity is present only when both male and female are represented.

The grounding of the sex of the Deity in either the female or the male gender is not simply a semantic issue. Rather, it also has significance in determining one's ethical system, how one perceives the material world, and the very meaning one sees in life and death. Thus, for example, in matriarchy, material creation is the model for all creation, and reality and value are found in the material world, while in patriarchy, reason is the model for all of creation, and reality and value are found in the nonmaterial world. As well as these primary characteristics in which matriarchy and patriarchy offer opposing views, they also oppose one another in secondary characteristics, such as matriarchy's valuing of settlement and the soil, in contrast to patriarchy's valuing of the nomadic life-style.[10]

Contemporary female and male religious understanding likewise often have different perspectives on key issues. Thus for example, men in conversation often express a greater concern for personal immortality than do women. Women seem to be more centered on birthing and life issues, while men concentrate more on nonbirthing and death issues. For women, redemption is often seen in terms of creativity, while for men, redemption is seen as being freed from sin. Sin itself is often experienced by women as self-abnegation, while for men, sin is usually equated with pride.[11] What these different perspectives would seem to call forth is not the advocacy of one viewpoint and the rejection of the other, but rather an understanding that honors both perspectives.

What is called for is a breaking out of the patriarchal model of the Trinity into a model that honors the feminine experience of life—both human and Divine. How might we do this?

Joseph Bracken suggests that

> the biggest roadblock to a proper recognition of the feminine in God is surely the traditional relationships of origin used to describe the genera-tion of the Son from the Father and the spiration of the Spirit from both the Father and the Son. Within such a scheme there is no natural place for a feminine principle.[12]

In order to overcome this seeming impasse, Bracken would suggest that the relationships of origin be looked upon as only one of the many possible relationships which exist among the three co-equal Persons who make up the Christian Trinity. In order to do this, the analogy of the Trinity as an interpersonal community, rather than as a family, is called for. With the interpersonal community analogy, the feminine aspect of God/ess could be investigated, not just in the Holy Spirit, but in the Son and the Father as well. Traditionally, the Spirit has been seen as the bond of love which exists between the other two Persons; this might be characterized as Her/His feminine side. But in an interpersonal community, the Father may also be seen as the bond of love in Her/His relationship to the Son and the Spirit, and the Son seen as the one who mediates between the Spirit and the Father. Thus is revealed the feminine side of both the Father and the Son. Bracken states that the possibilities for exploring the feminine in each of the three Persons is endless if one uses the communitarian mode.[13]

While not treating of the issue of the feminine in the Godhead, Jürgen Moltmann does offer insight into the issue of the relationships of origin. He does this by looking at the New Testament and finding that the relationships of origin are just one of the many relationships depicted there among the Father, Son, and Spirit. He would see these patterns as applicable not only to the Trinity and its relationship to creation but as intrinsic to the life of the very Godhead.[14] Thus, for example, in the sending, delivering up, and resurrection of Christ, "the Father is the actor, the Son is the receiver, and the Spirit the means through which the Father acts on his Son and the Son receives the Father."[15] However, if we look at the Lordship of Christ and the sending of the Spirit, we find that the Father and the Son are the actors, while the Spirit is the receiver. But when we consider the eschatological dimension of history, the New Testament shows us that the Spirit and the Son are the actors while the Father is the receiver. Moltmann points out that, in the West, only the first pattern has traditionally been used as a model.[16]

While Moltmann here does not treat directly of the feminine issue of the Divinity, he does examine the feminine issue when he looks at the Father as the exclusive source of the Son. He reasons that:

> If the Son comes forth from the Father alone, then this coming forth must be thought of as both "procreation" and "birth." But this means that there must be a fundamental change in the father-concept. A father who both *begets* and *gives birth* to his son is no mere male father. He is a motherly father. He can no longer be defined as single-sexed and male, but becomes bisexual and transsexual.[17]

Moltmann sees the above as the point being made by the Council of Toledo, held in 675, where the Son was defined as being "from the womb of the Father" *(de utero Patris).*[18]

Abba

What the statement issued at the Council of Toledo seems to indicate—that the source of the Godhead transcends human begetting and birthing—may be better understood by us if we referred to God/ess as both Father and Mother. In our private prayers—and in our public worship—addressing God as Mother/Father would make us aware not only of the personal care which the Creator lavishes on all of creation, but also deepen our understanding that this Creator transcends any human model we have ever experienced.[19] Being free to address God as Mother would also enable those who have had experiences of a loving female parent but no such experiences of a loving male parent, to be open to the possibility of a caring Deity. If, in fact, we do not mean that the Deity is male when we use masculine images and pronouns, what would be the basis for objecting to the use of feminine images and pronouns in our limited human attempts to describe that which is beyond description? Some would bring up the issue of our tradition and Scripture, but there is more at stake here. (Otherwise, how does one account for the following experience? When I speak to groups on the Holy Spirit, people are able to look at their experience of the Spirit and use, to everyone's approval and comfort, such images as Yardstick, Lamp, Bird. But I can count on one or more people becoming extremely angry if I suggest the image of the feminine for the Spirit.) If we don't mean male when we say Father-Son, then why not, as, for example, Elizabeth Johnson suggests, use Mother-Daughter as well?[20]

While I strongly suspect, based on my personal experiences, that the deeper question here is not intellectual but psychological, as a theologian I will have to limit myself to addressing the issue of the exclusive use of the Father image for God/ess. In our own time, this usage appears to be defended in large part because of the research done by Joachim Jeremias on Jesus' use of *Abba*. Based on Jeremias's research, it has become generally accepted that *Abba* is unique to Jesus and central to his understanding of the Deity. However, further research has brought these findings on *Abba* into question. Thus Joseph Fitzmyer, in researching the question, says that he has found no clear evidence to substantiate the understanding of *Abba* as an informal and intimate form of address.[21] And in a recent address to the Catholic Biblical Association, Madeleine Boucher questioned the centrality of *Abba* to Jesus' understanding of the Deity and to his prayer. She noted that there are only four texts containing *Abba* which can be considered authentic to Jesus, and, of these, only one is in the context of prayer (Matt. 6:9; Luke 11:2).[22] Furthermore, G. F. Moore has shown that "our father in heaven" was neither unique nor original language, but rather was the religious idiom characteristic of the culture of Jesus' time.[23] And finally we must consider the question of whether "Father" is the best translation of *Abba*. Jesus' use of the word, and the meaning that has been attached to the word *Father* through the ages, lead H. Paul Santmire to conclude that "Father" is not the best translation. He postulates that for Jesus, *Abba* was a mother-father figure, whereas for us, God the Father has become the sustainer of the patriarchal system. He suggests "Our Parent" as a more adequate and appropriate translation of *Abba*.[24]

In addition to reassessing the meaning of the *Abba* experience, contemporary scholars have also looked into the question of concentrating exclusively on one word, *Father,* to describe the experience of Transcendence. While we may no longer fashion golden calves as objects for worship, we do not seem open to the fact that language can be as much or even more idolatrous than the creation of such images.[25] In other words, any one word or image (for example, Father), if used exclusively, can become idolatrous in that its exclusive use would indicate that it is capable of containing the totality of who the Deity is.[26] A comparison may be made here to the naming of the animals and the naming of woman by Adam in the Genesis story. This naming may be termed false in that "inadequate words have been taken as adequate."[27] These words are by definition inadequate because woman was not a part of the naming process. So, for women today, to exist humanly means to name God/ess as well as the self and the world.[28] Only an

adequate naming can bring about the re-creation of a world that cries
out to be born anew.

The *Filioque* Clause

Whereas Joseph Bracken cites the positing of the origin of relationships
exclusively in the Father as the chief obstacle to discovering the feminine
principle in the Deity, the *filioque* clause may also be viewed as detrimental to this discovery. This is specifically the case if one is attempting
to develop a theology in which the Holy Spirit is seen as the feminine
aspect of the Godhead. In Western Christianity, we have a dual problem:
not only have we not developed a theology of the feminine in God/ess,
we have also not developed an adequate theology of the Holy Spirit.
This latter may be a consequence of the *filioque* clause, which may
be looked upon as evidence of subordination of the Spirit to the Son,
or, as one theologian has expressed it, the subordination of the creativity
principle to the reality principle.[29] The critical nature of this issue calls
for a thorough examination of the history of the *filioque* clause, as
well as its present status in the West. Within the scope of this chapter,
we will have to limit ourselves to a brief overview of that history and
status.

To begin, it should be noted that the Biblical evidence justifying the
filioque is slight and comes mainly from one source, John.[30] Furthermore,
the *filioque* was not part of the original Niceno-Constantinopolitan
Creed. It first came into use in Spain in 381. Its use was then spread
by Charlemagne and finally by Pope Benedict VIII.[31] We find that the
filioque was omitted in the recitation of the Creed in Paris as late
as 1240.[32] Based on the preceding historical evidence and on the discussions conducted by the Commission for Faith and Order at its ecumenical
conferences in 1978 and 1979, Moltmann makes the following summary
concerning the *filioque* clause: only the Father is the origin of the Godhead; the Spirit cannot proceed from the Father and from the Son
because, if this were the case, there would be two origins in the Godhead.[33] The *filioque* is "a later addition to the credal text of an ecumenical
council which was itself only recognized as such at a late stage."[34]
It is an interpretative formula. As such, it can be withdrawn.[35]

This movement toward rejoining Eastern Christianity by returning
to an ancient creed is not confined to the World Council of Churches;
there is also evidence of a similar movement on the part of Roman
Catholicism. Thus, in 1988, while participating in a liturgical celebration
with Orthodox dignitaries, Pope John Paul II made the decision to

go back to the fourth-century form of the creed, which does not contain the *filioque*.[36] These actions on the part of the Western church hierarchies may be viewed as evidence toward the freeing of the Holy Spirit and finally, after almost two millennia of neglect, the opportunity to develop a comprehensive theology of the Holy Spirit. In such a theology She would no longer merely be honored on occasions such as Pentecost and the conferring of the sacraments of initiation; rather She would be experienced as a living presence in the life of the churches and by all Christians. Presently some theologians are moving toward freeing the Spirit and writing about Her as a coequal member of the Trinity who is radically free and creative in Her own right. This idea is expressed well by Jay G. Williams:

> The Spirit may proceed from the Father but is in no way subservient to him. She is the life of the Godhead; it is she who goes out (proceeds) so that the hidden Pantocrater is made known. In the divine economy, it is not the feminine Person who remains hidden and at home. She is God in the world; moving, stirring up, revealing, interceding. It is she who calls out, sanctifies, and animates the church. Hers is the water of the one baptism. The debt of sin is wiped away by her. She is the life-giver who raises men [*sic*] from the dead with the life of the coming age. Jesus himself left the earth so that she, the intercessor, might come.[37]

A Gender-free Model of the Trinity

Another way to treat the feminine Divine is through the development of a theology that looks at each of the Persons in the Trinity in gender-free terms. Such a trinitarian theology has been developed by, for example, Marjorie Hewitt Suchocki. For Suchocki, the revelation of God/ess takes place at two levels: general revelation, which is God/ess's witness in the natural world; and special revelation, which is God/ess as seen in history (for the Christian, specifically in the history of Israel and of Jesus). The second type of revelation may be characterized as redemptive in that it addresses the distortions caused by sin.[38]

General revelation—how God/ess is revealed in the world through our own consciousness—occurs in three ways. One is the human experience of loneliness, or spatial alienation, that can lead us to the experience of God/ess as *presence,* a presence that is loving. Second, the human experience of insecurity, or temporal contingency, can lead us to the experience of God/ess as *wisdom,* a wisdom that elicits from us a response of trust. Third is the human experience of injustice, a societal experience that can bring us to an understanding of God/ess as *power,* a power in which we can hope. The first two experiences of God/ess take place in response to individual problems, while the third answers the societal issue of justice.[39]

In addition to her understanding of revelation as the basis for her theologizing, Suchocki also maintains that theology must be grounded in a philosophical framework. She finds this necessary for two reasons: because relationships with God/ess are more often found at preconscious rather than at conscious levels of existence, and because a philosophical structure can prevent theological statements about God/ess from being simply wishful statements based on human needs.[40]

Using her grounding in process theology, Suchocki characterizes God/ess (as well as all such other modes of reality as humans or stars) as an actual entity, that is, a drop of experience which comes into existence through the creative process of becoming.[41] Actual entities may be defined as the final realities that make up existence.[42] Viewed as such, the Deity transcends the human category and is not subjected to anthropomorphism. Thus, by viewing God/ess as an actual entity, the process theologian is free to view the Divinity in gender-free terms, namely, as Power, Presence, and Wisdom.[43]

Suchocki maintains that our human experience does more than reveal God/ess as Presence, Wisdom, and Power for us. Our human experience also leads us to an understanding of God/ess's own nature. This is so because the Deity cannot be less than the Deity can do; "the cause must be sufficient for the effects."[44]

In developing her ecclesiology, Suchocki presents an understanding of the Wisdom of God/ess as that which creates, sustains, and guides the church. This role is the role traditionally ascribed to the Holy Spirit.[45] But Suchocki develops her understanding of the Wisdom of the Divinity within the context of process theology. Thus, "the effect of God's wisdom is that no matter what threats and contingencies we may experience, God is faithful to lead us into a creative mode of dealing with these problems."[46] This occurs because God/ess feels each experience in the world as God/ess's own experience. For example, God/ess experiences my pain as pain, my joy as joy, the insentient experience of a rock as insentient, and so forth. God/ess integrates this feeling knowledge into the depths of the Divine Being and offers it back to the world as that which is redemptive, faithful, and creative Wisdom.[47]

Likewise, Suchocki's understanding of God/ess as Presence may be seen in terms of the availability of the Deity to us through every moment of our existence.[48] When Suchocki develops her understanding of the Divine Presence in the processive mode, she would see this role fulfilling that which is ascribed to Jesus Christ.[49] In the context of process theology,

the Divine Presence is both our source and our destiny. As beginning
and end,

> God not only begins our existence through the touch that mediates possi-
> bility to us, but God also feels us at the conclusion of each momentary
> existence, integrating that which we have chosen to become into the divine
> awareness.[50]

The Divine Presence directs us "toward an optimum mode of existence
in the world."[51]

Suchocki's understanding of God/ess as Power is grounded in an understanding of the nature of Divinity as being the power for justice.
As such, God/ess is both the source of the vision and the reality of
the just society.[52] Suchocki's development of God/ess as Power shows
Power to be equated with the One whom traditional theology has usually
called Father.[53] The Divine Power has two aspects: it is both self-creative
and transitional, that is, capable of influencing others. As self-creative
Power, God/ess is the locus and the unification of all possibilities. However, because God/ess as Power is One, the possibilities themselves can
only be good. As transitional Power, God/ess makes the possibility of
a just society achievable. However, whether this possibility is actualized
depends on the response of the world to that which God/ess as Power
offers to it.[54]

Furthermore, Suchocki contends that the terms *Wisdom, Presence,*
and *Power,* are more appropriate for describing the Trinity today than
are the terms *Spirit, Son,* and *Father.* This follows because the latter
have lost the meaning they originally held. Thus, for example, the word
Abba was used by Jesus to describe an intimate relationship whereby
the Divinity's Wisdom was conveyed to him. Through this intimate
communication, Jesus was enabled to be the one who did the work
of God. Today, by contrast, the term *Father* connotes male progeneration.
Likewise, the term *Son* once spoke not so much of the maleness of
Jesus but of the inclusiveness of the Incarnation. Today, however, we
emphasize the maleness rather than the inclusiveness. Spirit originally
conveyed the Wisdom of God/ess in the ordering of the church, but
this precision is lost to the contemporary world and the word *Spirit*
has taken on a diversity of wide-ranging meanings, including that of
maleness.[55]

In summary, it may be said that while Suchocki starts from general
revelation and develops her theology in processive terms, she ends by
presenting a trinitarian theology which she sees as faithful to special
revelation. A question remains as to whether, insofar as she does not

deal specifically with the gender issue, she will enable women to grapple with the issues that most concern them today (such as that of self-concept).[56]

Overcoming the Dualities

The above-mentioned models of theologizing have looked upon the Deity as object rather than subject. However, in both theology and worship, there are examples of meeting the Deity as subject. While these examples do not treat the issue of the feminine in God and are generally not specifically trinitarian,[57] they should be mentioned because of their value in helping us overcome some of the dualities that need to be healed today, such as that between object and subject or that between person and cosmic power.

In her article "Naming God in Public Prayer," Mary Collins has suggested that the sole normative biblical revelation of the Divine Name is that given to Moses, *YHWH*. She draws that conclusion because, in its ineffability, it is the only name that takes seriously enough the First Commandment, against the prohibition of idols.[58] Collins would also see "I am" as the decisive name for the Deity in the Fourth Gospel.[59]

Again in the context of worship, Miriam Therese Winter also addresses the Divinity as subject rather than as object. Rather than singing of the Spirit in the third person, she writes:

> Spirit of God, ev'ry one's heart is lonely,
> watching and waiting and hungry until,
> Spirit of God, we long that You only
> fulfill the earth, bring it to birth and blow where you will.
> Blow, blow, blow till I be
> but breath of the Spirit blowing in me.[60]

While the context may be different, this treatment of the subject-object question is echoed in Indian religious experience. In this instance, the discussion begins specifically with the issue of the gender of God/ess, that is, whether the Deity is to be regarded as She or He or It. The Indian experience indicates that the Deity is all three and beyond all three. Further, it may be argued that, if the Deity is always subject and never object, then the only true name is "I."[61] (This would be similar to Mary Collins's findings on the scriptural naming of the Judeo-Christian experience of the Transcendent.)

A further dichotomy, this one evidenced by the trinitarian theological models presented in this chapter, shows those models as representing

two opposing categories: those which, like Joseph Bracken's, see the
Deity in personal terms, and those which, like Suchocki's, see the Deity
in cosmic terms. However, for some theologians this is a false dichotomy.[62] It may be argued that it is not necessary to use anthropomorphic
symbols for naming the Transcendent, and that nonpersonal language
can truly express the Judeo-Christian experience of the Divinity. For
example, rather than using a noun as either subject or object, Mary
Daly suggests that we view God/ess as a verb, as "Be-ing."[63] God/ess
as Be-ing would offer many possibilities for theologizing, particularly
in processive terms, but might prove difficult to integrate into the worship
experience.

The Evaluation of the Trinitarian Models

Within the trinitarian context, we have presented three kinds of models: that of the Holy Spirit as the feminine Divine (chapter 1), the
androgynous model, and the gender-free model. I would now like to
speculate on how these models may develop in the future. While I
would anticipate that all three kinds of models will probably be developed more or less concurrently, their development does seem to call
for a certain logical order.

The first priority I see is a comprehensive theology of the Holy Spirit
as the feminine Divine. It is possible that Christianity has never developed
along pneumatological lines because of its inadequate understanding
of the nature of the Holy Spirit: we have never lived with Her in depth
as the feminine aspect of the Deity. Now that that understanding, and
people who are trained to express that understanding theologically, are
available, we may anticipate Her receiving the time and adoration which
are Her due as a coequal member of the Trinity. For this to happen,
however, we must be free to view the source of the Godhead not simply
as Father but also as Mother and possibly, in a communitarian model
rather than a familial one, as "the One who calls the community into
Being." Further, as Leonard Boff suggests, we must be open to the
notion of the divinization of Mary through her relationship to the Holy
Spirit as the feminine parallel to the divinization of Jesus through his
relationship to the Word.[64] We must also develop images that move
beyond Irenaeus's image of the Word and the Spirit as the two hands
of God/ess. At this point in time, one of the most powerful images
available to us is that of a three-faced carving representing the Deity.[65]
This image speaks of the oneness of the Divine, as well as of its triunity
and duality. The duality of the Divine is expressed through the feminine
and the masculine—there is much material for meditation in such an
image.

Our second type of trinitarian model is the androgynous model, in which the masculine and the feminine are present in each of the three Persons of the Deity. Much work and sharing of experience must take place before we are able to see ourselves as androgynous, let alone come to an understanding of what this means for the trinitarian Persons. It would seem that a first step must be for women to gain an in-depth understanding of the feminine. As this self-definition on the part of women evolves, humankind will be better able to elicit the meaning of the feminine in the male, as well as the meaning of the masculine for both sexes. In other words, it seems that humankind will need to go through an explicitly feminist phase before achieving general competence to treat the issue of androgyny in ourselves or in the Divinity. However, there are theologians who are already personally competent to work in this androgynous model. One may build on the insights of Joseph Bracken or, indeed, on Andrei Rublev's icon of the Trinity, which was produced in the early fifteenth century. The androgynous nature of the three Persons in Rublev's icon is apparent to the eye. The possibilities for contemplating the relationships of origin is also made apparent by the disagreement among Orthodox theologians as to which figure represents the "Father."[66] The possibilities for using such images are vast.

Our third type of trinitarian model used gender-free langauge for the Deity. For some, theologizing in this manner is seen as a way of avoiding the whole gender issue. Nonetheless, it may be that this model can present us with some powerful images which can help us to grow in our love and understanding of God/ess. Thus, for example, we may consider Suchocki's image of the Holy Spirit as Wisdom. Although the term *Wisdom* has for many a passive connotation, a more active sense is conveyed by Webster's, which defines *wisdom* as "the faculty of making the best use of knowledge, experience, understanding, etc."[67] This definition involves three parts: the objective (knowledge, understanding), the subjective (experience, judgment), and the faculty, or power, of using the first two elements.

When Wisdom is seen as Power women—and men—are encouraged to develop this virtue and see it as an active rather than passive way of being. This also enables us to see the Holy Spirit not as passive, but as a Wisdom which is creative and world renewing. Further, if Mary Daly is correct in her perception that the personal/cosmic power dichotomy is a false dichotomy,[68] theologians will be freed to develop trinitarian models with such terms as Wisdom, Presence, and Power.

The issue of the gender of God/ess may seem to be an esoteric issue in a world where three time bombs—the economic, the environmental, the nuclear—tick inexorably toward detonation. However, some of us have been grasped by the certainty that, until we change our images of God/ess so that the feminine Divine is available for our worship and theology, there are no ultimate solutions that will save Mother Earth and her inhabitants.

"We become what we worship: for we worship that to which we aspire absolutely and ultimately."[69] The honoring of only those values given to us by a patriarchal culture are no longer sufficient. We must also incorporate the values of the feminine or we will perish, having experienced only half of the meaning of our creation as female and male in the image of the Holy One.

Chapter Five

The Feminist Mystic/Prophet

In revealing God/ess, the religious feminist movement makes an invaluable contribution. Our challenge is to grasp the extent to which this revelation radicalizes our experience of the spiritual journey. Our understanding of conversion is being reexamined. Personal experiences of the Divine, once the domain of otherworldly mystics, are being grounded in a spirituality of the earth. Our commitment to social action is being translated into prophetic ministry.

In the first part of this chapter I will explore the meaning of conversion in two ways: first, as the call to embrace the feminine and to commit ourselves to those oppressed who embody the feminine: namely women; second, as the necessity of integrating our lives through the power of a spirituality that understands mysticism/prophecy as interwoven threads of a single cloth. In the second section of this chapter, I will discuss four models of this integrated spirituality that are part of the heritage of the mystical tradition. These models are drawn from the works of Julian of Norwich, Mechtild of Magdeburg, Meister Eckhart, and Hildegard of Bingen. In the last section are the writings of six women—Jill Harker, Clare-Marie Anderson, Beth Fitzgerald, Ellen Bechtold, Mardy Cribbin, and myself, that briefly describe a moment in their religious experience. Overall, this chapter is intended to serve as a touchstone for an ongoing dialogue, bearing witness to an emerging revisioning of what religious conversion might mean in the twenty-first century.

Conversion: A Feminist Feminine Consciousness

A central aspect of spiritual growth is the experience of *metanoia:* a never-ending and never-easy story speaking of change, inner intrinsic change, a change of heart. A feminist perspective seeks a liberation that goes beyond *merely* personal God experiences into a deeper consciousness; as a reimaging of person(s) intimately related to creation—not

97

as a by-product of conversion but as the very fiber and core of the journey itself. Creation is the stuff of the universe, be it in the form of stardust, water, whale, or human. Since women are regarded as both *mater* ("mother") and matter, a woman's spirituality calls upon a God/ess capable of such inclusion. We are called therefore not only to reimagine ourselves and our place in the cosmos, but to reimagine our God/ess as intimately revealed within this cosmic story. It is the naming of this experience that empowers, transforms, and, indeed, re-creates us as mystics/prophets.

The method and fulfillment of the mystical way has been greatly influenced by persons with an introverted perspective. The classic journey inward is frequently described as stages of growth toward God—often associated with "purgation," "dark nights," and an occasional glimpse of joy. God is experienced as transcendent and/or immanent, and necessarily as "Other." In this model, the mystic struggles to remain faithful to this "Other" as Lover or as Truth. The journey culminates in union with God, transforming the human psyche in a blissful state of working for and with God in all one's daily activities. The direction of one's life, particularly in Western cultures, frequently turns to the marketplace, to reentering the world, perhaps as a reformer of society. However, emphasis is also often placed on personal disciplines and mystical experiences, giving the impression that mysticism is "otherworldly."

Feminists and other liberation theologians find something lacking in this scenario, namely, the universe. From their perspective, our inner journey is a movement into the universe and into a God/ess of the universe, a broadening of consciousness and perception that transforms individualistic attitudes into cosmic connections with cosmic responsibilities. We must reclaim our passion for a life-giving God/ess reflected in human creative energies.

The conversion that God/ess calls us to, therefore, requires a new freedom and way of being that gives birth to compassion, an abiding with and within which honors mystery, pain, and paradox. Compassion aptly imaged and known to be integral to our understanding of motherhood is expressed in Hebrew in related root words: *rehem* and *rahamin*. We know that our first experiences of being mothered indelibly predispose us, to a greater or lesser degree, to our sense of self-worth and trust. For nine months each of us was held in maternal darkness. "Mother" is the first and primary trusting bond of our lives and the source of constant nurturance and love. This birthing power, though obviously a gift of women, refers also to the birthing power within men and all creation as well. As children, it is Mother-God we cry for, the "from everlasting" maternal acceptance and belonging that stirs us so deeply. We long for Her as She longs for us. She has been revealed: "I groan like a woman in labor." (Isaiah 42:14) But this revelation has not been honored as a central theme of the Judeo-Christian tradition. In the call to conversion, the fleshy heart we must personally embrace is the heart of our maternity. God/ess as compassion is also our unconditional lover and dark trust, aspects women have known in their hearts long before written history. Since women have been culturally encouraged to develop themselves as nurturers, and since women can celebrate in their own bodies cosmic connections, it is no surprise that women's spirituality reflects a God/ess experience inclusive of body, birthing, and cosmos. Indeed, our first godly images were of fertility. Most men, disassociated from their own birthing and nurturing powers, have clung to fear and domination in a desperate attempt to stamp out vulnerability and insecurity. The new consciousness dawning today allows the healing of this deep wound for both women and men. As women reimagine that which is feminine as being inclusive of strength, purpose, and personhood, men conversely are reimagining that which is masculine as being inclusive of intimacy, vulnerability, and interdependence. No longer must women create only with their bodies; no longer must men create only with their minds. As this evolving convergence comes to term, human consciousness revisions and reimagines itself as whole and healthy—indeed, as blessing.

While holding this integration for humanity as a vision that will bring about a positive future, I insist that this vision, no matter how exciting and hopeful, must be carved out of our daily endeavors and will not be born without the labor required of every birthing process. We are the foremothers of the twenty-first century, in hard labor, struggling to birth a feminist feminine consciousness. The experience of women, revealed in a spirituality and psychology that reflects this reality, must be told: "herstory" created for the first time. The conversion from God to God/ess is, in large part, a conversion into this feminine consciousness expressed in images of creativity, freedom, and compassion, and naming intimate personal and cosmic interdependencies. The God/ess requires a new cosmology. As futurist and ecologist Thomas Berry has stated, it is the emerging cosmos herself that immediately reveals that which is Holy. We are called to not only envision ourselves in new ways, but that newness must embrace the whole of the universe and our relationship to the cosmos. A feminist perspective automatically extends itself beyond the personal into the prophetic affirmation of matter. This requires a different stance in our God/ess relationship: not the stance of a child, but that of co-creator—the stance of responsible and empowered adults who have Divinity running through their veins.

The Mystic/Prophet

Feminist mystics then, standing in the mystery of their own personal and cosmic experiences, in awe and in silence, must somehow bear witness to what they have experienced. Their responsibility and unique gift is to articulate life experiences of the Ineffable: the numinous, diaphanous union of the divine and the human. In the extremely difficult task of putting into words the "groaning of the Spirit" they strain for expression. It is not that they are unclear or uncertain, just impossibly limited in expressing that which is more than merely rational, that which is essentially Mystery. This condition is common to the mystic way, as Evelyn Underhill so clearly states: "There is no certitude to equal the mystic's certitude: no impotence more complete than that which falls on those who try to communicate it."[1]

Despite this apparent difficulty, the mystic contributes immeasurably to human development because the mystic can be "a pioneer of humanity, a sharply intuitive and painfully practical person: an artist, a discoverer, a religious or social reformer, a national hero, a great active among the saints."[2] Within the archives of the mystical tradition are examples of women and men involved in the integration of passive and active states, efforts of intense personal prayer interfaced with rigorous social involvement, as exemplified by Hildegard of Bingen and Meister Eckhart. But this integration has been largely localized in just such individual people and not embraced as one of the core purposes of mystical experience. The tradition has been, I believe, affected by a tendency to accent "the passive state," as reflected by the influence of Quietism. The tradition has also been greatly influenced by a search for perfection that often entails extreme ascetic practices.

If the goal of mystical experiences were expressed as compassion rather than perfection, I suspect that the prophetic dimension would be considerably more fundamental and evocative. I suggest that the thrust for the return to the marketplace be made manifest through an embodied spirituality both exposed and energized by the prophetic work of justice-making that is more than a call for social reform. The prophet calls for systemic change, a change possible only with the reevaluation of our assumptions and categories that perpetuate injustice—not simply a reshuffling of old pieces but a real inversion of power.

The prophetic dimension of the journey story is as significant and integral to our conversion as is the mystical. The mystic and prophetic are two interfacing aspects of the same conversion process, providing a balance of inner and outer, and making integration possible. Claiming ourselves as prophets means first and foremost claiming ourselves as persons of a passionate God/ess, for without deep passion no newness of life is possible. We must find what profoundly moves us, where our creative energies lie—it is likely that there resides also our vulnerability, our inner pain, our place of bondage. It is here we find God/ess, mingled within our pain, for the prophet's only hope is that "the *ache* of God[/ess] could penetrate the numbness of history."[3] This sacred eros compels us to create new life options, to dare to imagine the not yet. This is the central work of the prophet: "to keep alive the ministry of imagination, to keep on conjuring and proposing alternative futures"[4] by continually naming the heretofore unmentionable pain and offering alternatives. This is exactly what feminists have done and continue to do through consciousness raising and herstory. Allowing myself to enter the pain, anxiety provoking though it is, is the only way to process what ultimately transforms into creative futures. "The riddle and insight of biblical faith," suggests Walter Brueggemann, "is the awareness that only anguish leads to life, only grieving leads to joy, and only embraced endings permit new beginnings."[5]

Major spokespersons of God/ess's fecundity today, therefore, are those who struggle to allow the painful emergence of a feminist consciousness "that can energize the community to fresh forms of faithfulness and vitality."[6] Feminists, through their use of language, image, and ritual, have recovered feminine symbols that evoke a critique of the existing male-dominated religious systems and simultaneously offer new possibilities and hope to an emerging community of believers. This enables women and men to embrace the darkness of personal and collective letting go while concurrently creating a deepening passion for new life-giving possibilities and integration. My prophetic stance is in dialogue with my mystical experiences. No longer must we be either mystics or prophets: now we can and must claim our experience both of God/ess and of the call to bring about justice as two interweaving threads of one common experience, the experience of the mystic/prophet. An introverted mysticism is a truncated mysticism and a mere social reformer is no prophet at all.

Our prophetic dimension resides in our ability to dare to image that which to date has been unimaginable in flesh-and-blood terms. For feminist mystic/prophets of the Christian tradition, a central question remains: Have we been so spiritually and psychologically abused by a misogynist culture that we are incapable of imagining a viable belief system that honors femaleness and androgyny? Specifically, is the institutional Roman Catholic Church convertible? Even as Christian churches ordain women, name the sin of sexism, make efforts at inclusive language for worship, the question remains: Can Christianity fully embrace the feminine/female experience theologically, psychologically, and spiritually? Will institutional Christianity ever dare to proclaim the feminine Divine? And if it is not capable of doing so, can it survive? It is not just religious institutions that need converting. Nor is it just individual persons who endure and give birth to feminist consciousness. Our culture, reflected in its economic, political, social, and educational interactions, is in grevious pain. Our call as feminist mystics/prophets is not the call of the elect but rather a latent intuitive response to the intrinsically equalitarian and political Divine. It is our center, where God/ess resides with our passion, pain, creativity, and connectedness. In absorbing Her message, we come to grasp afresh the meaning of prophetic mysticism. We are called to a life-style open to mystery, responsible and compassionate living, and the making of justice for all of God/ess's people, beginning with the *anawim,* God/ess's "little ones," the forgotten, marginalized, and powerless.

As we enter into dialogue with the *anawim* and see ourselves revealed in them, we come to know the meaning of interdependence. Our faith response must be embodied in social realities. This is the fulfillment of the journey: to bring to reality God/ess's vision, a vision of inclusion through compassion. Union with God/ess drives me out into the world. I am propelled not just to bring about equality, but to do so *not* from my own personal viewpoint but from God/ess's viewpoint, from my mystic/prophet experiences of union within the heart of God/ess. Liberating prophetic voices are the union of the mystic/prophet, our call to create an embodied godly presence in our culture through justice. No longer can we afford the luxury of dichotomizing our God/ess experiences into the "active" and the "passive," into God/ess pursing us or our pursing God/ess. Ever we are the pursued pursuer. the sought-after seeker.

The embodiment of God/ess's viewpoint requires political, economic, and social redistribution of power. "Prophetic faith denounces religious ideologies and systems that function to justify and sanctify the dominant, unjust social order."[7] The call for justice must be inclusive of women as normative for society. This is primary and nonnegotiable.

> Feminism goes beyond the letter of the prophetic message to apply the prophetic-liberating principle to *women.* Feminist theology makes explicit what was overlooked in male advocacy of the poor and oppressed: that liberation must start with the oppressed of the oppressed, namely, *women* of the oppressed. This means that the critique of hierarchy must become explicitly a critique of patriarchy. All the liberating prophetic visions must be deepened and transformed to include what was not included: women.[8]

Thus, those searching for new world vision—economically, politically, religiously, ideologically, racially, ethnically, and ecologically—must re-examine themselves in light of womanhood. Do such revisions simply rearrange male power? Is "male" still the assumed norm (language, metaphor, and resistance are good indicators of this)? Are we to *assume* (as with the "generic," term *mankind*) that women are included? A truly radical—that is, rooted—conversion is possible only when we are converted at our core-self that always touches our identity as enfleshed persons and, hence, as sexual beings. Anything less is incomplete and unsatisfactory.

Practically speaking, this conversion will require a shift in power, better designated as empowerment. Personal *metanoia* ("Seeing myself in a new way, I am *called* to the transformation of myself"[9]) is balanced with a response to the *anawim*, the oppressed.

> Conversion, to the extent that it includes not only a transformation of individual persons but an invitation to participation in a wider community of being, carries with it a charge to share the vision that actualizes power as it is newly apprehended. Conversion thus becomes a force for social revolution.[10]

This revolution is neither anarchy nor women's superiority nor violent takeovers. This is the "new heart" revolution, the bringing about of justice, the power of God/ess integrated into our lives.

> We must create a living pattern of mutuality between men and women, between parents and children, among people in their social, economic, and political relationships and, finally, between humankind and the organic harmonies of nature.[11]

A journey consciously aware of the feminine requires us to embody the meaning of relationship. This is an especially humanizing gift, natural to all of us, and the crying need of our age. Women have been too narrowly defined as care givers, and many are struggling to expand their attitudes and grow into a deeper understanding of personhood. However, we humans have so lost our relational abilities that we are in danger of undervaluing and thereby undermining all relationships in our society, to the point of planetary holocaust. This breakdown of our capacity for intimate and genuine relationship is endemic in a dualistic system that "opposes soul, spirit, rationality, and transcendence to body, flesh, matter, nature, and immanence. God is identified with the positive sides of the dualism, and 'the world' with the negative sides."[12] This splitting of ourselves in two has ushered in an age of extreme anxiety and alienation in which we project all we do not understand onto an enemy who thereby represents evil. This model has shaped our ideologies, politics, and economics—indeed, our whole culture. Particularly targeted as untrustworthy, along with all of the rest of creation, have been women. "Classical dualism also became the model for the oppression of women when the culture-creating males identified the negative sides with the women over whom they claimed the right to rule."[13] And so we continue our violence. Only a small step is necessary for a society that systematically oppresses women and the feminine to move from the rape of women to the rape of Mother Earth. While the first *may* sometimes be caused by individual emotional disturbance,[14] the second is caused by collective political insanity and fear. What's more, our belief system has supported this destructive behavior. A supposedly Christian interpretation of the Genesis story has been the backbone of such dualistic thinking, by encouraging man to dominate the earth while consistently blaming Eve for sin. Is it possible for us now to celebrate her deep desire for an ever greater understanding of our divine roots, possible only through an upsurge of consciousness known as free will. As world powers compete to consume the tree of life and death, once again it is a feminine consciousness that considers other options. The affirmation of the feminine has stimulated dialogue for an ecologically responsible technology. Women and men who are in touch with themselves as nurturers, gardeners, and cultivators of life on this planet seek to protect Mother Earth from human devastation; they invite us to love our planet. Thomas Berry and many others rightly affirm that there can be peace among the nations only once there is peace with the earth. And there will be no peace with the earth until the human species establishes peace with the feminine, and those who embody the feminine, women.

The Christian Mystical Tradition

Along with contemporary explorations of God/ess images, symbol, and panentheistic worship, some degree of "establishing peace with the feminine" can be found in the Christian mystical tradition. In eras past much of the mystical tradition supported a body/soul split, frequently punishing the body to the benefit of the soul, reflected in various sadomasochistic behaviors. Nonetheless, in the pursuit of a new religious future, mystical theology is "the greatest support the tradition can give us on the long road to liberation and emancipation."[15] This is evident not only because mysticism is grounded in personal experience and therefore beyond official teaching authority, but also because in this tradition women have been able to respond fully to their God/ess experiences and be directly involved in the formation of others: religious women of the Middle Ages could find a

> sphere of activity, of self-expression, even of authority and jurisdiction, that stands in sharp contrast to the limited picture of the woman found in formal theology, legal structures of church and society, and the reality of patriarchal marriage.[16]

Once more, the naming of our spiritual lives as both mystic and prophet integrates women's experiences immediately because this inclusive perspective does not separate body from spirit or body from body politic. In the next sections, I will present four examples that exemplify this perspective.

Julian of Norwich

Highly honored in the mystical tradition is Julian of Norwich (1343–1419), a mystic of great depth who offers hope and encouragement for today. Several "signs of the times" today coincide with those of Julian's era: due to political unrest, new linguistic forms were introduced; illness, natural disasters, and unemployment were common; a spirit of legalism pervaded the church; the laity, due to better education and a new sense of social justice, became disenchanted with church authority. Julian's work, with its keen awareness of sin, is nonetheless filled with hope and affirmation. The continuing goodness of creation is emphasized, along with God's healing compassion.[17] Lastly, and most importantly for our purposes, Julian emphatically proclaims the Motherhood of God.

Mystics realize through experience what theologians articulate as articles of faith. Of the doctrinal issues Julian considered, the most relevant for contemporary insight is her insistence on speaking of God as Mother. Although traces of the maternity of God can be found in the work of other mystics—Saint Bridget of Sweden and Saint Catherine of Siena, for example, none speak in trinitarian terms with Julian's clarity and harmony. Julian asserts five characteristics of Divine Motherhood: it is expressed in imagery which is embracing, inclusive, exuding warmth and acceptance; it is intimately related to compassion and the bringing about of compassionate living; it involves birthing and all the labor associated with birthing; since all creatures are birthed by God, God is revealed in all creation; God Our Mother is expressed as Wisdom, reflecting the imagery of the Hebrew Bible.[18]

Julian approaches the Motherhood of God with rich metaphor and poetic grace, expressing a theology of trinitarian life inclusive of

> a description of God's *praxis,* of the offices and services of a mother toward her children, as he fulfilled them in his Son, Jesus Christ. He gave us life, his life, in his Incarnation and in his death. He nourishes us through the preaching of the church; he makes us grow through his grace, adapting himself to each of us in his infinite love.[19]

Through this synthesis, Julian offers us her experience of the total mystery of God. She clearly offers a model for proclaiming the Motherhood of God. Her words are grace-filled and profound in their simplicity:

> As truly as God is our Father, so truly is God our Mother. . . . To the property of motherhood belong nature, love, wisdom and knowledge, and this is God. . . . We have our being from him (Jesus Christ), where the foundation of motherhood begins, with all sweet protection of love which endlessly follows. . . . The mother can give her child to suck of her milk, but our precious Mother Jesus can feed us with himself, and does. . . . I understand three ways of contemplating motherhood in God. The first is the foundation of our nature's creation; the second is his taking of our nature, where the motherhood of grace begins; the third is the motherhood of work. And in that, by the same grace, everything is penetrated, in length and in breadth, in height and in depth without end; and it is all one love. . . . I am he, the power and goodness of the fatherhood. I am he, the wisdom and lovingness of the motherhood. I am he, the light and the grace which is all blessed love. I am he, the Trinity. I am he, the Unity.[20]

Thus, with great beauty and profound sensitivity, Julian expresses what today must be heard. It is encouraging to know that a woman of such depth and grace has gone before us.

Even though these descriptions of Mother Jesus provide a model of love and compassion, and a real honoring of women by associating this with God's action, to me it is also problematic. Essentially, the mothering is still in "his" terms; it is attributed to a male person, Jesus. There has been no clear distinction in Christian thought between Jesus of Nazareth, Jesus the Christ, and the Spirit of Jesus: all are considered in male terms. Thus, nurturing qualities are attributed to this male, allowing for integration; women can appreciate this, yet they are only secondarily affirmed. Since there is no acknowledgment of feminine Divine Presence, no normative female counterpart exists.[21]

The attitude toward women as somehow "less than" is evidenced by the mixed response to the American Episcopal Church as it installed its first woman bishop. The Anglican and Roman churches still refuse to ordain women. However, significant though it may be, ordination, by itself, is not enough. To a large extent, women, particularly laywomen, still remain passive observers. Perhaps this will remain so as long as the feminine Divine is denied. It is possible that further theological study would free us from a restricted historical male Jesus image, and would thus give birth to a deeper penetration into the mystery of resurrection. Perhaps further psychological study would help us understand the roots of misogyny in a culture that disenfranchises half of its population.

Central to this issue is the timely prophetic statement of Julian's message: the bringing about of justice for women and men in naming themselves as imaged after a God who is very much our Mother. While this is not the only image women refer to today, and while it does not encompass all the facets of God/ess, nonetheless, the image of God as our Mother is a significant move toward wholeness. It is, perhaps, the first stirrings of feminist awareness.

In a similar vein, Michael Mott, biographer of Thomas Merton, recalls Merton's mention of his overwhelming love for people experienced during a visit in Louisville. Searching Merton's original journals, Mott discovered that this experience referred specifically to Merton's love toward women: he was really seeing women as people, apparently for the first time, and he loved them. This new awareness for Merton, while not complete, was an insight into the feminine. His need for the feminine in God, according to this private journal, was related specifically to Julian of Norwich's theological genius and the revelation of Jesus as our Mother.[22]

The imaging of God in feminine terms will also bring about liberation by helping to balance an unchecked distorted Father image prevalent in today's Christianity. This has direct implications for women. "By the ability to identify in gender with God, women are raised to a new power as human beings."[23] Women can begin to understand themselves in godly terms, while men can begin to let go of an excessive identification and enter more readily into God/ess as mystery. Clearly, this would be reflected in men's relationships with women, affirming women's intrinsic dignity while reflecting God/ess's image.

Mechtild of Magdeburg

We now come to a less well-known thirteenth-century mystic, Mechtild of Magdeburg (1210–1280), another source for feminist mystical theology. We encounter here a woman of depth, commitment, and sensitivity. "All her longing and struggling, as also her peace and joy, her freedom and independence, were founded on [the] experience of God in her own being."[24] It is to make this claim that women still struggle today. Her confrontation with the church resulted in her being treated, as so many before and so many since, as a heretic. Nonetheless, she exerted great influence on such key contributors as Dante and Eckhart.

Mechtild affirms our Mother God as One who welcomes us warmly on Her breast and protects us from harm, "as swiftly as a mother lifts her darling child from the ground to her knee."[25] Remembering our childhood, our times of maternal comfort, we too can perceive the Trinity in womanly terms. Mechtild speaks of herself as soaring into God "as a child finds itself under its mother's cloak and lays its head on her breast."[26] As long as we have one such memory, we can know implicitly this Mother God—and what better image to foster for those of us deprived of such tranquility. Surely this Mother God can transform human rejection into trust and security.

While depicting the soul as Queen, Mechtild is quick to embody her experiences. "Love melts through the soul into the senses, that the body also may have its share, for it [love] is drawn into all things."[27] No dualistic separation acceptable here! Indeed, Mechtild perceives God panentheistically, in all sacred matter, and bursts into poetic ecstasy:

> O lovely rose on the thorn!
> O hovering bee in the honey!
> O pure dove in thy being!
> O glorious sun in thy shining!
> O full moon in thy course!
> From thee I will never turn away.[28]

We can hear the words of a later mystic, Pierre Teilhard de Chardin:

> Crimson gleams of Matter, gliding imperceptibly into the gold of Spirit, ultimately to become transformed into the incandescence of a Universe that is Person—and through all this there blows, animating it and spreading over it a fragrant balm, a zephyr of Union—and of the Feminine.[29]

Panentheistic honoring of the sacred is equalitarian wonder, intrinsic to mysticism: "Touching a stone or a tree, drinking water and milk, being with fire or standing in the wind or listening to birds. Seeing the parts, realizing the whole, connecting inner and outer."[30]

Inherent to Mechtild's experience is her natural integration of prophetic witness. The essence of her journey is not private ecstatic experiences but healing through compassion. We are called to imitate our compassionate God/ess; She is clear in her demand. The bringing about of justice to the oppressed, whom I earlier referred to as the *anawim,* is not optional. Rather, it is the fulfillment of our journey. "If you love the justice of Jesus Christ more than you fear human judgment then you will seek to do compassion."[31] Perhaps if we rested on the lap of our Mother God for ten minutes daily, the courage to live compassionately would be ours. The more we live within this God/ess, the stronger would be our passion for life giving. If herstory were to be told, if women were to be honored, celebrated, and affirmed, women's conscious awareness of interdependence would cultivate a Christianity of compassion rather than a Christianity of rigidity and patriarchal oppression. With the oppression of women has come the oppression of all feminine expressions, expressions that could be life giving for us all.

Meister Eckhart

A mystic of unspeakable depth, Meister Eckhart (1260–1328) is another major contributor to our understanding of the integration of the mystic/prophetic experience open to feminine imagery. Myriad books have been written about Eckhart, but in this brief discussion, I will focus on only two themes in his work: birthing and compassion.

We have in Eckhart an image of God/ess as birther. God/ess does not create externally, as if watching from afar the results of Their creative moment. Rather, God/ess creates passionately, intimately: with "the kiss of the soul, there mouth comes to mouth,"[32] giving birth within us to God/ess's word. As mystic/prophet, I cannot say I speak of God/ess; rather, God/ess speaks of God/ess within me. God/ess revelation is personal, involved, intimate, forever creative and creating.[33] All creatures, including human creatures, coming from, imaged after, our Birther God/ess! How healing, how empowering! We are connected, interdependent, interrelated, intimate birthers of goodness, blessing, gift waiting to be shared. This proclamation of equality of being and sacredness of all creatures is panentheistic, allowing for a deep reverence for life.[34] At the same time, this is an experience beyond naming, where, finding God/ess, we find ourselves. Our divinization, then, is a sinking into this darkness, beyond our knowing, into wisdom, silence, and mystery.

Thus, our journey stretches us not into formulations and metho-
dologies but into a simplicity-complexity of the natural flow of life.[35]
Our journey is both knowing and not knowing, darkness and light,
birther and borne. The earth reveals this to us in the natural course
of day and night. (Since we enjoy electricity, we have extended our
daylight and have decreased the natural darkness. Thus we feel we have
control over our lives. But that control is artificial and untrue.) Our
inner being knows both the darkness and the light. Both must be re-
spected. Metaphorically, our Sun God and Heavenly Father must be
integrated again with our Moon Goddess and Earthly Mother.

In Eckhart, the feminine Divine spirals through compassion into the
prophetic work of justice-making. In his sermon "Our Divinity and
God's Divinity: To Be God Is to Give Birth,"[36] we witness the new
life possibilities of a spirituality in touch with birthing ourselves, each
other, our planet, our God/ess. For just as God/ess gives birth, we
too are called to birth God/ess with our lives. On this Divine-Human
mutuality rests our identity, as well as our fulfillment. This mutuality
is anchored in love, a love that requires equality and unity, the works
of compassion, the doing of justice.

For those who would cling to a personal "God and me" spirituality,
Eckhart is abundantly clear: "We ought to get over amusing ourselves
with raptures for the sake of a greater love which is to minister to
what people most need, whether spiritually or socially or physically."
For a God/ess who "waits on human history and suffers as she waits"[37]
compels us to action. Compassion is not theory but action.

On our journey into compassion, however, we do begin with ourselves,
our personal story, our personal wounds, our personal needs. It is from
this beginning place we venture out, learn to risk, learn compassion.
It is not possible any other way. "Love your neighbor as you love yourself" requires a healthy self-valuation and self-nurturance that honors
body, psyche, and spirit as an integrated whole.[38] When I live with
a healthy self-respect I can know that I live in relation to you and
I can perceive a depth of oneness that embraces grief as well as joy,
weakness as well as strength, poverty as well as abundance. To know
this in our heart is know that when we save the whale, we save ourselves;
when we enact a new international economics, we save ourselves; when
we work for social justice, we save ourselves. The interdependencies
that many women have longed for are here, not only recognized but
honored. In the breakdown of the barriers between us, we birth compassion, we birth love, "for love will never be anywhere else than there
where equality and unity are."[39] I believe this is the equality and unity
that women are struggling to express, an empowering truth of our inti-

mate interconnectedness, our mutuality in relationship as well as responsibility, our integrity as persons created in Her image. Wedged against the prejudicial assumptions of church and state, women's claiming of their own integrity, their own naming, is in itself a prophetic statement. For the bringing about of the reign of God/ess in human herstory is the bringing about of the compassionate living that justice-making women are challenging us to embrace, beginning with themselves as the "oppressed of the oppressed."

When we let go of our sense of exclusivity, of life as a possession we control, or an "ownership mentality,"[40] God/ess can take over. Our prayer life becomes an "our" consciousness, a consciousness that is not satisfied with personal spirituality out of touch with the reality of the poor. The "poor" are the *anawim*, the powerless, patronized, ignored, and feared people of our society. The "poor" are attitudinally viewed as less than normative, unacceptable and marginalized. The "poor" cross-culturally are women!

Thus an integrated mystic/prophetic spirituality reveals a conversion story which flows freely from the personal to the transpersonal, announcing a God/ess experience of freedom, creativity, and compassion available to all.

Hildegard of Bingen

The last touchstone we shall consider for our grasping the meaning and depth of mystic/prophetic experiences is Hildegard of Bingen (1098–1179). Firmly rooted in the creation-centered tradition, she was a multi-faceted, gifted woman, an artist, scientist, and mystic who embodied and thereby expressed an integrated spirituality that names a personal, interpersonal, and cosmic experience of Divine union. The key to her work lies in the meaning of relationship. All of creation is held in perfect harmony and balance. This is God/ess's justice concretized in holy matter. "With my mouth I kiss my own chosen creation. I uniquely, lovingly, embrace every image I have made out of the earth's clay. With a fiery spirit I transform it into a body to serve all the world."[41] This is the original Wisdom, the original blessed event from which our universe continues to emerge. It is the Holy Spirit breathing life into matter, God/ess's continuing creation of the universe.

And so life will bloom when there is justice, that is, where there is integration and balance. This mutuality among creatures is commonly understood as the balance of nature, which is vulnerable to human indiscretion. We must confess to the obvious condition of imbalance within ourselves and our relationships, be they among women and men, international economic and political systems, national spending patterns, or in our treatment of Mother Earth. We know that people suffer today from a profound sense of fragmentation and disintegration. We are manipulated and governed by greed and fear. This is injustice and, therefore, an enemy of godliness. Our need to bring about unity and balance calls us immediately to justice making.

This personal/interpersonal/cosmic rupture, the source of dualistic thinking and acting, is clearly portrayed by Hildegard as sinful. She relates a creation story in which God is a flame and we are a little clod:

> The flame is making the clod warm because the earth is the material from which the flesh of people is made. The flame is nourishing the clod, just as a mother nurses her child. This flame breathed into this body and blood, and a person was brought forth. . . . The person did not smell the flower with his or her nose, nor taste it with his or her mouth, nor touch it with his or her hands. This means that the person followed God's command with the understanding of wisdom—as if with the nose, but the person did not allow the strength of God's command to enter him or her completely—as if in the mouth. Nor did the person do his or her work with the fullness of blessedness—as if with the hands. But this person left and fell into a very dense darkness.[42]

The darkness here is the dark confusion and meaninglessness suffered by those who refuse to enter into life fully, who separate themselves from their own creative abilities, cosmic connectedness, and divinity. It is a fracturing of the Divine relationship, a breaking away from this feminine energy source, this nurturance that brings forth life and sustinence. It is denying, marginalizing, or trivializing our Divine image.

We are being challenged to be imaginative and creative, to reclaim our Divinity: "O foolish people, who were made in the image and likeness of God, how can you abide without trying out your image and likeness?" questions Hildegard.[43] Surely our creative energies could at least *imagine* a world of justice, a church that does not oppress its people, a political order capable of an alternative to violence and destruction! We are called to trust our dreams and not be overwhelmed, for we have the capacity to alter our reality, to widen our options, to persevere for the sake of justice. And to seek wisdom.

The life-giving image for our journey is a circle, for in a circle persons are peers and leadership can easily flow. Honesty, mutuality, acceptance, and forgiveness are possible. This maternal God symbol must be personally experienced if we are to receive Her blessing and be enabled to celebrate Her presence in our midst. Clearly, if this image was proclaimed and our anxieties were allowed to rest in this Mother God, we would receive a new source of Divine Energy, a deeply rooted gift of trust— poignantly absent in our present world view as well as in our daily encounters and relationships. We have Hildegard to remind us: "God hugs you. You are encircled by the arms of the mystery of God."[44] The prophetic voice affirms these personal hugs as deep and authentic only when we are willing to risk our place of comfort and peace in order to embrace one another. Our circle must remain open to receive. Thus we give birth to compassion and justice, the fruit of our godly roots that calls us to bring balance into our lives and our relationships.

Our conversion story must be radical. This requires letting go of our prejudices that humans are to control other humans or other species at will, that humans are not accountable to the planet. Clearly, this kind of living would not abide racism, sexism, militarism, ageism, classism, or economic and political oppression. Hildegard's theology is based on an interdependent and intimately connected cosmology, not a flat world of up and down, either/or, us and them. Our journey, honoring the ebb and flow of our lives, requires a framework or spiritual- ity that integrates, stimulates, and envisions afresh what it means to be human. We cannot separate God/ess and cosmos, or our religious experiences into exclusive categories of mysticism or prophecy, soul or body. Our prayer moments happen not when we mentally decide to pray but when we choose to remain open and therefore experience God/ess happening. The stirring of new life possibilities is the bringing about of justice in our relationships and deeds. This is the *viriditas* (greening power) Hildegard offers to us as the healing power that saves. "The Holy Spirit is greening power in motion, making all things grow, expand, celebrate."[45] Our greening power is reflected neither in our being "green with envy" nor in the "power over" of our greenbacks, but in the fertile greening of our psyche, body, and spirit that saves, values, shares, enjoys.

This life-giving greeness, combined with "judicial fire, burning up the injustice of sin,"[46] comprises for us both the personal mystical experi- ence and the prophetic cosmic voice to stand, in trust, opposed to inequalities however demonstrated—be it disregard for women and the feminine in our daily encounters institutionally, socially, and personally or disregard for creatures of Mother Earth and the emerging cosmos. And as befits the dignity of the human species, it is love, compassionate love, that makes this possible. This embodiment would bring about a surge of creative energy and compassionate power that would be life giving for this planet. Given today's circumstances and "life and death" options, Christianity must integrate in this fashion if it is to survive—indeed, if any of us are to survive.

Women Today

The bringing about of justice for women and men and the integration of the feminine in our consciousness is a primary godly movement intimately related to who we are and how we hope to live in the twenty-first century. Key to this understanding is a fresh look at our personal, interpersonal, and cosmic relationships. It is the emergence of a new culture whose God/ess continues to birth new possibilities.

Honoring these new possibilities are six women who have contributed reflections on their personal journeys.

Prayer Reflection on the "Our Father"
by Jill Harker

dear woman
who I am part of,
wisdom is your name.
Your justice comes
Your truth is done
on earth as it is inside me.
You are with me today
in my daily work
and enliven my dancing
and we enliven those
who dance their music.
With you my acts are
free from lying
and my body free from numbness,
and mine is the healing,
and the power and the peace.

MY CREED
by Clare-Marie Anderson

I believe—
In Divine Energy,
Source of all energy.

I believe—
>	In mystery, wonder, and creation.

I believe—
>	In the Oneness of the Cosmos.
>>		The eternal connection with all that
>>			Was, Is, and Ever will become.

I believe—
>	In the Universal Spirit,
>		the Breath of Life, the Vital Center.

I believe—
>	In motion, change, and process.

I believe—
>	In shared responsibility,
>		In shared growth,
>			In shared gifts.

I believe—
>	In drinking in the fruits of the earth.
>		In revitalizing the earth.
>			In our rootedness in Mother Earth.
>			In our connection with and
>				Communion of all the Cosmos.

I believe—
>	In the Eternal Now.
>		The timelessness of time.

I believe—
>	In AT-ONE-NESS.

I believe—
>	In the reflection of all Beauty
>		As is incarnated in the Universe.

I believe—
>	We are of God/ess
>		in God/ess
>		with God/ess
>		for God/ess
>		as God/ess
>>			Alleluia!

Child's Play: Mother, May I?
by Bernice Marie-Daly

Mother may I?
Mother? Church Mother, may I take
three giant steps within?

No. No you may not . . .
"I baptize you priest, prophet, king."

Mother Church, may I take three giant steps within?
Mother? Mother Church, may I?
Mother! Church Mother, are you my mother?
Do you nurture life within me?

Mother!
Mother, Church Mother, I take
(Oh, please!) steps inward.
Giant three,
to name who you are within me.

Mother, my mother.
My giant Mother
Three steps—three depths
within me.

Mother, my God-Mother!
Must I take these
Your giant steps/depths within?

"*I* baptize you."

Mother, Our Mother
Our Giant Mother!
Three steps—three depths
within us.

Mother, Our Mother
Life giver/Life Sustainer: Creator.
Breathing Giant Birth Within
Granting Divine Naming
At-One-ness Personified.

Blessed Earthly Mother
Unrequited Lover
Wounded-Healer calling.

Goddess-Mother
We accept Your giant stepping
Compassion reclaiming, renaming

Freedom, depth within.

In The Moonlight
by Beth Fitzgerald

In the midnight hush I walked toward the ocean. There was a murmer of waves against the sand, a gentle breeze carrying the scent of wild roses, lights twinkling on the opposite shore, an amazing display of stars overhead, a full moon low on the horizon casting a shimmering silver path across the sea.

Suddenly my knees buckled, a strangled cry rose in my throat: "it is too beautiful!" I felt tears, my whole being seemed to flow out in agonizing gratitude, and I knew with utmost certainty that only a Mother could be so generous, could gift me so extravagantly. "Thank you, thank you," I whispered, and stood weeping in the moonlight.

Mother God
by Ellen Bechtold

Mother God loves me unconditionally. She knows of all my experiences. She knows of oppression for She, too, has been oppressed.

Every day I have quiet time with Mother God. I remember once sitting with Her on a rich brown dirt bank, next to a moving stream in the forest. Sometimes the stream moves fast and full, and other times it moves slowly and peacefully. Mother God and I sit there together for long hours, often just in quiet. In my daily life, frequently when I have painful or angry feelings, I have learned to return to this prayerful image. I tell Her of my difficulty. Sometimes She holds me in an embrace when the pain is too hard to even feel. Sometimes She holds my hand as we sit and I tell Her of my anger or confusion. Sometimes, when I am feeling pain from the scars of anorexia, I lay my body on the rich earth, with my head on her lap. Mother God hears me; She knows me and is hearing me into wholeness and being. I am learning to feel feelings as I believe they are meant to be, and to process them. I am learning to sit with my pain and sadness and joy; learning to be. I feel loved and that being a woman is Holy.

what kind of God are you?
by Mardy Cribbin

what kind of God are you? a God who bears
me gently in your womb, who births your life in me,
a God who nurtures me with you and shares
the songs of love's own harmony
with all creation. what kind of God are you?
a God who holds me in your very heart, who treasures me,
a God, a mother, who upholds me ever one in you.

Chapter Six

What Was, What Is, What Will Be

In the introduction, we spoke of the images and words we would present in this book as parts of the unfinished mosaic of the feminine Divine. We have now completed our presentation—a few pieces to be added to Her eternally evolving picture. These images have included the psychological, the theological, the mythical, and the mystical. They have come largely out of our Western Christian tradition. However, we have also moved out of our tradition, compelled by the fact that our primary reality is that of being woman; being Christian is a secondary reality. Thus we would look to the Feminine as our primordial source of revelation. The myths of patriarchy are not sufficient for women—or for men—in our own time, if indeed they ever were. Throughout our writing we have tried to show the implications for both the old and the new stories. Since we become what we worship, we think that how we image the Divine is the ultimate practical question.

The implications for how we image the Divine can be applied to our economic crisis, our peace crisis, our ecological crisis. However, because the feminist response to the environment seems to be, at this time, the most explicit, we will limit the remainder of our discussion to how the myths of patriarchy have brought us to our present ecological crisis and to some of the tools needed if we are to re-create the earth. We end with looking at the vision, for, if we can imagine it, then it can come to be. For we have the power to bring about a new way of being, if we will but cooperate with Her.

The Matricentric Age

We are privileged to live in a time when we can travel in word and picture back to the age before the stories of the Hebrew patriarchs. Indeed, scientific stories now take us back to within a fraction of a second of the beginning of our present universe, while the findings

119

of the archaeologists tell us about our ancestors who lived many thousands of years before our Scriptures were even part of an oral tradition. Taking these findings into account, we discover that the way in which the history of Western civilization is presented may no longer be viable.

A dramatic restructuring of the story of Western civilization is being called forth today. One way in which the story can be presented so that new data can be honored is by looking at Western civilization in terms of three historical periods: pre-patriarchy (6500–3500 B.C.), which ended with the Aryan invasions; patriarchy, which encompasses the past five thousand years; and postpatriarchy, the era now emerging, which may be identified as the ecological age, characterized by total participatory governance. These three periods can also be referred to as matricentric, patricentric, and omnicentric, with -centric indicating cultural integrity (in contrast to -archal, which indicates domination). The third age might also be called the eco-feminist age since the nurturing qualities and spontaneities needed at the present time are those usually referred to as feminine.[1]

One of the values to have emerged through our growth in understanding of the first, or matricentric, age, is that we now have the means whereby the whole of Western civilization can be reassessed. Thomas Berry states that the apparent success of the matricentric periods delivers a critique of the patriarchal period that is more profound than those delivered by secularists or Marxists.[2] He sees the driving forces of the critique as

> the rising consciousness of women and the devastation of all the basic living forms of earth presently taking place in consequence of the male-dominated regimes that have existed during this [patriarchal] period.[3]

What are some of the values of the matricentric period that stand in such sharp contrast to the values of the patriarchal age? For Riane Eisler, one of the primary values presented by the matricentric age is the lack of evidence of damage through warfare for a period of over one thousand five hundred years. In areas where warfare was not practiced, the Goddess was worshiped.[4] But this worship of the Goddess did not necessarily mean that there was domination of the male by the female. Rather, Eisler finds evidence for a partnership between the sexes rather than a dominator model. In such a model, diversity is honored, not superiority or inferiority.[5] This true honoring of diversity stands in sharp contrast to the genocide practiced in the patriarchal age. Further, Eisler takes Crete as an example where the partnership model was a lived reality. Here she finds evidence that the common good was valued above the wealth and power of a few individuals.[6] Finally, it must be stressed that this matricentric age—the age characterized by peace, partnership, and concern for the common good—was not an age characterized by lack of activity. Rather, it was the age that witnessed the development of law, government, medicine, agriculture, metallurgy, architecture, the wheel, pottery, textiles, and written language.[7] Unfortunately, this age came to an end, in Old Europe at least, through successive waves of invasion from the Russian steppes that occurred between 4500 and 2500 B.C.[8]

However one may view the matricentric age (and much more work must be done before a final judgment can be rendered), the evidence does seem clear that from circa 7000 B.C. (possibly as early as 25,000 B.C.[9]) to 500 A.D., our ancestors worshiped the Great Goddess much as people in the patriarchal age worshiped God.[10] In other words, there was another age before the patriarchal age. Patriarchy was not there in the beginning and thus there can be another age after patriarchy. In fact, patriarchy may be characterized as a five-millennium detour that occurred after thousands of years of partnership.[11] How does one characterize this detour through whose painful ending we are now living?

The Patriarchal Age

For Sheila D. Collins, the structure of patriarchy is seen as resting upon four interlocking pillars: racism, class exploitation, sexism, and ecological destruction. She analyzes patriarchy in terms of unjust relationships, citing sexism as the paradigm from which the other three are derived. She reaches this conclusion because sexism is the first and the longest lasting of the unjust relationships.[12] However, it can be argued that there is a mind-set that undergirds and makes possible all four unjust relationships: the hierarchical mind-set that legitimates all forms of exploitation in regard to the entire Creation.

By contrast, Thomas Berry analyzes patriarchy not from the point of view of unjust relationships, but in terms of unjust institutions. He sees Western history as presently controlled by four establishments: classical empires, the ecclesiastical establishment, the nation-state, and the modern corporation.[13] As a result of their actions, we are presently witnessing "the closing down of all the basic life systems of the planet."[14]

While all four establishments need to be explored, given the orientation of this book we will focus on the ecclesiastical structure. Especially pertinent here is Collins's characterization of the patriarchal world view of this structure. For Collins, this world view consists of: the fall from grace, the need for humanity to be saved by one from outside through obedience and submission ("death to the old self and rebirth to the new in Jesus Christ"), and pride as the basic sin.

A fatal flaw of this world view is that it deals only with the personal and not with the political. It sanctions the status quo, for to question the divinely established boundaries is equated with committing sin. It suggests that social evil will be overcome if there are enough individual conversions. Ultimately, it leaves one hopeless in the face of social evil.[15]

This issue of the personal and the political will be explored in some depth later in this chapter, but for now our characterization of patriarchy can be summed up with Berry's observation that:

> The sense of *patriarchy* has now evolved as the archetypal pattern of oppressive governance by men with little regard for the well-being or personal fulfillment of women, for the more significant human values, or for the destiny of the earth itself.[16]

It is not enough to describe the patriarchal structure of society as it exists today. If we are to change that structure totally, we must understand the historical process that initially brought it into existence.[17] It appears to be rooted both in biology (sex) and in culture (gender).[18] Evolutionary biologist David P. Barash sees patriarchy as ultimately determined by the fact that males "produce many small, relatively cheap gametes."[19] Furthermore, since certainty in paternity is very difficult to determine, males tend toward behavior that is competitive, aggressive, and promiscuous. They tend to dominate their mates through terror in order to lessen the possibility of being cuckolded; males value generation more than caring for their offspring. Females, by contrast, produce few, but relatively large and expensive gametes. Sexual intercourse is not the activity of a moment's duration as it is for the male, but often results in a prolonged period of gestation, nursing, and child raising. Maternity is certain, and each offspring is singularly important.[20] Elizabeth Dodson Gray would also find the need to prove oneself to be peculiar to the male and to be located in his "envy of the female's sense of intrinsic worth which needs no proving and which is based upon childbearing."[21]

However, it is not only sex (the biological), but also gender (the cultural) that enables patriarchy to perpetuate itself as a system. Ultimately,

> the system of patriarchy can function only with the cooperation of women. This cooperation is secured by a variety of means: gender indoctrination; education deprivation; the denial to women of knowledge of their history;

the dividing of women, one from the other, by defining "respectability" and "deviance" according to women's sexual activities; by restraints and outright coercion; by discrimination in access to economic resources and political power; and by awarding class privileges to conforming women.[22]

But if women have historically functioned in ways that perpetuated their own oppression, today we have the historical conditions to enable us to bring about our own emancipation from subordination. The first condition for this transformation is to free ourselves from the patriarchal framework that has conditioned our very being.[23] This coming into freedom will necessitate the risk of questioning that which cannot be questioned, namely, the sacred, which is perceived as the unquestionable answer to all questions. This questioning, which is already underway, by its very nature produces the psychic shock we are presently experiencing.[24] This is so because what is being questioned is the revelatory experience itself, as well as the classical humanism that undergirds Western civilization.

If the foundation falls, the structure cannot remain in place. Yet this is precisely what must take place, for it has become apparent that the system does not need merely to be modified—it needs profound change. What we must assent to is the basic principle governing every revolution: the rejection of all partial solutions. Only when the root cause—patriarchy—becomes evident will change take place. In addition, the experience of change must be perceived as less painful than the experience of continuing on as is.[25]

The pain in which most of creation is presently living is such that many are willing to undergo the pain of radical change. However, those who recognize that they are in pain must have a new vision that will enable them to create a new world. And those who are in pain without recognizing their true condition must be brought to awareness of the true state of Creation, including humankind. This bringing to awareness is being accomplished particularly today by the eco-feminists with their insights into the earth-human condition.

The Eco-Feminist Critique

The eco-feminists may be defined as those who see the link between the domination of women and the domination of nature.[26] This insight is based on the number of striking parallels that exist between the treatment of nature and the treatment of women. For example, the traditional role of both women and nature is seen as an instrumental one, that is, both are seen in terms of their usefulness to others rather than as having intrinsic worth in their own right. Also, each occupies a sharply differentiated place in the hierarchical system.[27]

The parallels eco-feminists have discovered between the treatment of nature and that of women echo the insights of Lynn White, Jr. In his article on Christianity as the historical source of the Western ecological crisis, White observes that, "Especially in its Western form, Christianity is the most anthropocentric religion the world has seen."[28] It "not only established a dualism of man and nature, but also insisted that it is God's will that man exploit nature for his proper ends."[29] "By destroying pagan animism, Christianity made it possible to exploit nature in a mood of indifference to the feelings of natural objects."[30] White further thinks that our ecological crisis will continue to worsen unless we explicitly "reject the Christian axiom that nature has no reason for existence save to serve man."[31] Since White sees the source of the ecological crisis as religious, he would see the solution being of necessity religious.[32] In summary, while White does not explicitly make the connection between the exploitation of nature and the exploitation of women, he does see the problem in terms of the categories of dualism and instrumentalism employed by the eco-feminists.

A leading eco-feminist proponent of the primacy of dualism as the root cause of the ecological crisis is Rosemary Ruether. She finds the crisis rooted in the creation of patriarchy in that patriarchy denied:

> that the spiritual component of humanity was a dimension of the maternal matrix of being. Patriarchy sought to elevate consciousness to supernatural apriority. Mother and nature religion traditionally have seen heaven and earth, gods and humans, as dialectical components within the primal matrix of being. Its spirituality was built on the cyclical ecology of nature, of death and rebirth. Patriarchal religion split apart the dialectical unities of mother religion into absolute dualism, elevating a male-identified consciousness to transcendent apriority. Fundamentally, this is rooted in an effort to deny one's own mortality, to identify essential (male) humanity with a transcendent divine sphere beyond the matrix of coming-to-be-and-passing-away. By the same token, woman became identified with the sphere of finitude that one must deny in order to negate one's own origins and inclusion in this realm. The woman, the body, and the world were the lower half of the dualism that must be declared posterior to, created by, subject to, and ultimately alien to the nature of (male) consciousness, in whose image man made his God.[33]

Ultimately, both human moral failure (which is identified with the female realm of "carnality") and the failure of nature to conform to the demands of the infinite transcendent God, call for their own destruction and the creation of a new heaven and a new earth. This Ruether sees as the logical conclusion to the patriarchal self-deception that falsely locates the origin of consciousness outside of the maternal matrix. Further, this dualism results in man regarding woman and nature as "other," thereby making a dialogue impossible; the only relationship possible is one of domination and subjugation.[34] This paradigm of exploitation characterizes our present economic patterns where the many—people and the earth—are used to benefit the few. Talk of expanding this pattern of unsustainable growth to include the many means in reality depleting the raw materials and poisoning the environment for the continued benefit of the elite while the poor only get poorer.[35] But the earth will not be mocked; she brings her own judgment.[36] Today we experience this judgment in the air we breath, the water we drink, and the food we feed our children.

While Ruether exemplifies those who see the source of the ecological crisis rooted in dualism, Carolyn Merchant represents those who see the root cause in instrumentalism—the objectifying and use of the other for one's own purposes. For Merchant, there is an association between woman and nature that has persisted in culture, history, and language, and that is grounded in a world view which may be characterized as egalitarian. Nature and women are further linked by the ancient thinking that regarded nature as a nurturing mother.[37] Today, both women and nature are viewed as "psychological and recreational resources for the harried entrepreneur-husband."[38]

Before the scientific revolution, according to Merchant, nature was viewed in two contradictory ways: she was both a benevolent female and a wild uncontrollable one. After the scientific revolution the second image became the dominant one. This image of nature as wild and uncontrollable led to two key concepts: that of mechanism and that of domination.[39] In other words, for Merchant, the scientific era was "the crucial period when our cosmos ceased to be viewed as a organism and became instead a machine."[40]

> The image of the earth as a living organism and nurturing mother had served as a cultural constraint restricting the actions of human beings. One does not readily slay a mother, dig into her entrails for gold or mutilate her body. . . .[41]

When the earth was considered to be a living organism, it was treated within an ethical contest.[42]

In Francis Bacon (1561–1626), "the Father of Modern Science," Merchant finds explicated the analogy of the exploitation of both nature and woman. Thus, for example, the interrogation of witches served as a model for the interrogation of nature and the torture of witches through mechanical devices as a model for the torture of nature by mechanical means.[43] Nature came to be viewed as a system of dead particles moved by external forces rather than as a living system that generated its own movement. This mechanical world view enabled the most far reaching effect of the scientific revolution to become possible, namely, the death of nature. The death of nature was brought about by the new mechanical order and the values associated with it: power and control.[44] In this new world view, nature was no longer the teacher; rather, the human being became the measure of all.[45]

But it would seem that nature—and woman—are not yet totally dead. Rather, they are fighting back and doing this in partnership. Daly refers to this phenomenon as "the Great Refusal of rapism," which includes the "refusal to rape earth, air, fire, water, that is, refusal to objectify and abuse their power."[46] Daly continues:

> More than this, it means that the covenant embraces our sister the earth and all of her nonhuman inhabitants and elements. It embraces, too, our sisters the moon, the sun and her planets, and all the farthest stars of the farthest galaxies. For since they **are**, they are our sisters in the community of being.[47]

Earth and the other planets are being with us, not being for us. "One does not rape a sister."[48]

But along with the need to integrate, that is, to experience all of creation as a unity, we also have a need to differentiate. For while we acknowledge that all of Creation is united in that each being is simply a unique expression of life, we are also aware of our differences. The question is, Can we honor these differences in categories other than that of "power over"? Or, as Elizabeth Dodson Gray suggests, Can we think in terms of difference without the necessity of superiority? Our criterion for superiority is often rather one-dimensional. Yet, logically, if it is strength that is chosen as the measure of superiority, why are we not outranked by the elephant? Or why does not photoplankton outrank human life, since all of life depends on its oxygen-making powers while it can get along very well within the human element?[49] Gray concludes that we have based our modern life-style on the linear (male) while neglecting the cyclical (female). Thus, our reality is that

whether it is a sewerage system or an industrial production line, men
have created arbitrary and linear systems in vast conceptual disregard
of the fact that the world is based upon circular flows and functions
in vast systems of recycling.[50]

We can no longer afford the luxury of dishonoring the cyclical. Rather,
we must develop life-styles wherein differences are valued and seen
as part of the dialectical tension through which the fullness of life
is created.[51] Perhaps we are guilty of integrating where we need to differentiate (for example, seeing "man" as encompassing the totality of humankind) and of differentiating where we need to integrate (for example,
divorcing the personal and the political). Yet, if we are to move to
the new way of being, we must recognize the unity that does exist
between the political and the personal.

The Unity of the Political and the Personal

In Western Christianity, there has been an emphasis—one might say
an overemphasis—on redemption, while the doctrine of Creation has
been neglected. One is left wondering, after being redeemed, what there
is to do—besides wait for the Second Coming. However, the enormity
of the present-day situation, in regard to individuals, to nations, to
the very earth itself, has caused Christians to realize that they are called
to do more than save their own souls. They are also called to change
the unjust structures that are responsible for needless suffering in this
world. The contemporary Christian experience is that of the discovery
of the basis for change in the Scriptures, in such stories as Exodus
as well as in the teachings of the prophets and Jesus.[52] According to
Ruether:

> The claim that redemption in Christ has a social dimension has come
> about in modern Christianity only by an identification of its inherited
> messianic symbols with their secular interpretation in liberalism and social-
> ism.[53]

However, contemporary Christianity as a whole is hampered by the
counterclaim of some conservative Christians that redemption is purely
spiritual, not socioeconomic. However, Ruether insists that the creation
of the just self and of the just society cannot be separated. A large
number of converted people will not automatically cause a just society
to come into being; rather, the creation of a just society must be the

self-conscious act of committed individuals. Nor can one assume, as do the Marxists, that a just society will automatically create just individuals.[54] Rather, "we are engaged in a journey that is not only utterly individual, but also utterly communal."[55]

On a concrete level, what do spirituality and politics (the personal and the political) have in common?[56] Both politics and spirituality have to do with change. Politics may be regarded as the *what* of the process of change, while spirituality is the *how* of the process. Spirituality focuses from society to the individual, emphasizing the uniqueness of the individual; politics focuses from the individual to society, emphasizing the communal aspect. Spirituality emphasizes unity and connectedness, while politics emphasizes our separateness. In any process of change, there are three ingredients: an analysis of need for change (political); a vision, or belief that change is possible (spiritual); and a concrete plan of action (political and spiritual). In other words, the content of change is political, while the process is spiritual.[57]

In addition, both spirituality and politics share common ground in that both are concerned with power. This is:

> power created, maintained, and utilized in alignment with a particular view of life. . . . For instance, many people who function continually with unskillful, negative mindstates insist that human beings are naturally base and so require totalitarian policing. Hence, power over others can be built on ignorance, but eventually that ignorance and that kind of power can be dispelled by truth.[58]

Charlene Spretnak concludes by reminding us that, "We are building a revolution of the psyche as well as of the society."[59]

Hallie Iglehart finds the common ground of the political and the personal in their shared goal. This goal she sees as the creation of "a world in which love, equality, freedom, and fulfillment of individual and collective potential is possible."[60] In order to achieve this goal, the political and the spiritual must form a single unit.[61]

For some writers, however, the unity of the spiritual and the political lies deeper than a sharing of common goals or a grounding in power or in change. For, as Judith Antonelli points out, this perspective shows that it is necessary to work simultaneously on both the inner and the outer; what it does not do is challenge the idea that the spiritual and the political are two separate categories.[62] For Antonelli, the unity of the spiritual and the political "lies in the perception that matter is a manifestation of energy, that material reality reflects and symbolizes psychic reality."[63] Thus we may arrive at the feminist vision of spirituality which sees revolution as a psychic as well as a political movement, death as continuation rather than as obliteration, and, underlying it all, being as indestructible energy.[64]

Articulating the Vision

We have looked at the matricentric age and the patriarchal age. We have discussed the state to which the patriarchal mode of thinking has brought us, that is, the ecological crisis, and have examined the response of eco-feminism to this crisis. We have seen that if we are to respond creatively to the end of patriarchy, we must proceed in a way that is based on and acts out of the unity of the spiritual and the political. But one thing further is needed: this new way of being can only become a reality if we are able to articulate a vision. The articulation of this vision is the primary task before women—and men—who wish to join the Holy One in the new dance of Creation. Some would argue that the new ecological, or omnicentric, age can be brought about through reformation of the present system.[65] Thus, for example, both liberalism and socialism assume that women will be liberated when they are allowed to function like men in the public realm.[66] However, such thinking is based on the erroneous assumption that the patriarchal structure is both normative and functional. It is neither. For, as Berry points out, the old story no longer provides a context capable of endowing life with meaning.

For in fact, the old story broke down in the fourteenth century in the West with the coming of the Black Death. The response to that devastating plague was twofold: a movement by the religious community toward an understanding of redemption that would take us out of this tragic world and the formation of a scientific community that would enable us to escape the tragedy of this world by gaining control over it. These two divergent communities, the religious and the scientific, have been on opposing sides in our society ever since. But, in our own time, a new story is emerging which unites these communities. For we have become aware, through the emergence of human consciousness, that the psychic-spiritual has been part of the universe from the beginning. It is the role of the human to represent the moment in which the universe becomes aware of itself. The new story, based on a numinous, sacred understanding of creation, brings together the psychic-spiritual world of the religious community with the material-physical world of the scientist.[67] What is required of the religious community to make this story a reality is threefold: a sense that our primary revelation of the Divine is to be found in the sacred character of the earth itself; an understanding of ourselves as part of the process of Creation, with Creation itself being a psychic-spiritual, as well as a material-physical, reality; and a way of thinking and acting that honors the integrity of all of Creation.[68]

What is required of the whole earth community is that it act in a unified way to establish a functional relationship with the whole earth process. This interaction between the human and the rest of Creation must move beyond the recognition of national boundaries.[69]

But it is not only necessary that the human enter into the life process of the rest of Creation;[70] it is also necessary that the larger life community participate in our processes.[71] One place to begin this interaction between all the members of the total life community is within the context of ritual. We can employ new rituals to enable us to hear the voices of the trees, the rivers, the earth, the animals.[72] Or we can expand the context of our present rituals. Thus, for example, when we invite those who are not physically with us to join us in a particular place and time—to be "present"; we can extend this invitation beyond people to include the mountains, the tulips, the foxes, the beaches, the extinct species. We can welcome their presence, not only to our rituals, but to all our meetings—to be part of every decision-making process. For how can any decision be considered valid unless its consequences for the whole earth community are considered? People with special sensitivity to and knowledge of species other than the human could become their voices. It is not that the rest of creation is not speaking to us; it is just that most of us do not yet have the ability to understand their methods of communication. For the earth indeed speaks: through the polluted waters, the oil slicks, the eroded soils, the vanishing rain forests, the paved jungle. But the earth also speaks through the pounding of the waves, the hum of a bee, the individuality of a snowflake, the flight of a bird, the birth of a child.

It is not only to the voices of Creation that we must respond; we must also respond to the voice of the Creatrix. In order to hear Her voice, we must be willing to call Her by name. If we take that risk—if we learn to say the names of Goddess with the same total love and devotion with which we learned to say the names of God, we will find that we are not moving alone into a new world. Rather, we will awaken into a new community that has existed all along beside the old community.[73] In this new community there will be many familiar forms and faces, but also many which will surprise us. But, most of all, She will be there as She has been with Creation since the beginning. Accept her invitation; She is our bliss if we will but respond.

Notes

Introduction

1. See, e.g., Jürgen Moltmann, *The Trinity and the Kingdom* (San Francisco: Harper & Row, 1981), xiii, with whom we share the belief that "truth is to be found in unhindered dialogue."

2. Elizabeth A. Johnson, "The Incomprehensibility of God and the Image of God Male and Female," *Theological Studies* 45 (1984): 465.

3. See, e.g., Sandra M. Schneiders, *Women and the Word* (Mahway, NJ: Paulist Press, 1986), on why it is necessary for the spiritual growth of both men and women that the Divinity be imaged in feminine ways.

4. Mary Daly, *Beyond God the Father: Toward a Philosophy of Women's Liberation* (Boston: Beacon Press, 1973), 139.

5. R. M. Gross, "Steps toward Feminine Imaging of Deity in Jewish Theology," in *On Being a Jewish Feminist: A Reader,* ed. Susannah Heschel (New York: Schocken Books, 1983), 245. In this same article, see 238–40 for a powerful parody on role reversal when the Ultimate is portrayed not as male, but as female person.

6. In this case, we have used the word *human* rather than *male* because the latter is the assumed norm for both female and male humans.

7. Daniel C. Maguire, "The Feminization of God and Ethics," *Christianity and Crisis* 42 (1982): 59.

8. Yves Congar, *I Believe in the Holy Spirit,* vol. 3 (New York: Seabury Press, 1983), 155. In proposing this insight, Congar would appear to be relying on an honored understanding in rabbinical theology in which the form is compared to the Former.

9. Field Belenky, McVicker Clinchy, Rule Goldberger, and Mattuck Tarule, *Women's Ways of Knowing: The Development of Self, Voice, and Mind* (New York: Basic Books, 1986), 18.

10. Maria Harris, *Women and Teaching* (New York: Paulist Press, 1988), 17.

11. Rosemary Radford Ruether, *Sexism and God-Talk: Toward A Feminist Theology* (Boston: Beacon Press, 1983), 61, 69.

12. Ibid., 45.

13. Ibid., 45.

14. Clifford Geertz, "Religion as a Cultural System," in *Reader in Comparative Religion: An Anthropological Approach* 2nd ed., ed. William A. Lessa and Evon Z. Vogt (New York: Harper & Row, 1965), 206. However, it should

be noted that Geertz does not posit religion as the only symbol system. Others include science, common sense, and aesthetics (212).

15. Ibid., 213. Geertz sees ritual as the setting where this transformation occurs. Ritual is the place where the lived world and the imagined world are fused.

16. Gerda Lerner, *The Creation of Patriarchy* (New York: Oxford University Press, 1986), 219–20. See, Mary Daly, *Webster's First New Intergalactic Wickedary of the English Language* (Boston: Beacon Press, 1987).

17. Carol P. Christ, "Why Women Need the Goddess: Phenomenological, Psychological, and Political Reflections," in *The Politics of Women's Spirituality*, ed. Charlene Spretnak (Garden City, NY: Anchor Books, 1982), 77. Our methodology for doing thealogy finds expression in this article in which Carol Christ sees the symbol as the primary fact and the meanings as secondary. She bases her methodology on the insight that "symbols have a richer significance than any explications for their meaning can express" (77).

Chapter One: The Holy Spirit as the Feminine Divine

1. Yves Congar, *I Believe in the Holy Spirit*, vol. 3 (New York: Seabury Press, 1983), 155.

2. George Tavard, *Woman in Christian Tradition* (Notre Dame, IN: University of Notre Dame Press, 1973), 9–10.

3. Hos. 11:1–4, 8; Jer. 31:20; Isa. 49:14–16; Isa. 66:13.

4. Congar, *Holy Spirit*, 3:155. Readers interested in pursuing the feminine images of the Godhead in both Testaments are referred to, e.g., Virginia Ramey Mollenkott, *The Divine Feminine: the Biblical Imagery of God as Female* (New York: Crossroad, 1983).

5. D. F. Stramara, "El Shaddai: A Feminine Aspect of God" (Pecos, NM: Dove Publications), pamphlet.

6. Congar, *Holy Spirit* 1:3–4. An extensive treatment of the development of the theology of the Holy Spirit may be found in George T. Montague, *The Holy Spirit: Growth of a Biblical Tradition* (New York: Paulist Press, 1976).

7. Donald L. Gelpi, *The Divine Mother: A Trinitarian Theology of the Holy Spirit* (Lanham, MD: University Press of America, 1984), 45.

8. Montague, *The Holy Spirit*, 95.

9. Congar, *Holy Spirit*, 3:156.

10. Susan Cady, Marian Ronan, and Hal Taussig, *Sophia: the Future of Feminist Spirituality* (San Francisco: Harper & Row, 1986), 14–15.

11. Montague, *Holy Spirit*, 94, in reference to Prov. 1:23.

12. Congar, *Holy Spirit* 1:9. Wisdom is also identified as the Holy Spirit, e.g., Wisd. 9:17.

13. Ibid., 11.

14. G. F. Moore, "Intermediaries in Jewish Theology: Memra, Shekinah, Metatron," *Harvard Theological Review* 15 (1922): 55–58.

15. Raphael Patai, *The Hebrew Goddess* (New York: Ktav, 1967), 137–50.

16. Ibid., 157–60.

17. *Zohar*, trans. D. C. Matt (New York: Paulist Press, 1983), 55–56.

18. *Encyclopedia Judaica* 14 (New York: Macmillan, 1971), 1353.

19. A. Green, "Bride, Spouse, Daughter: Images of the Feminine in Classical Jewish Sources," in *On Being a Jewish Feminist: A Reader*, ed. Susannah Heschel (New York: Schocken Books, 1983), 257.

20. Joshua Abelson, *The Immanence of God in Rabbinical Literature* (New York: Hermon Press, 1969).

21. Congar, *Holy Spirit* 2:79.

22. E.g., 1 Cor. 3:16; 1 Cor. 6:19; Rom. 8:9; 11; Eph. 3:17; John 14:16–17; John 14:23; 1 John 4:12–13; 1 John 4:16.

23. Congar, *Holy Spirit* 2:81.

24. Gilles Quispel, "The Holy Spirit as Woman in Apocalypse 12" (paper delivered at the Patrological Congress, Oxford, 1979).

25. Congar, *Holy Spirit* 3:156. In the Gospels (e.g., Matt. 9:36, 20:34; Mark 1:41, 6:34; Luke 7:13), Jesus is described as being "moved in his bowels."

26. Montague, *Holy Spirit*, 135ff. For a development of the Holy Spirit as wisdom or enlightenment in the New Testament, see Gelpi, *The Divine Mother*, 50–60.

27. Elaine Pagels, *The Gnostic Gospels* (New York: Random House, 1979), 48–53.

28. Ron Cameron, ed., *The Other Gospels: Non-Canonical Texts* (Philadelphia: Westminister, 1982), 85.

29. Pagels, *The Gnostic Gospels*, 53–56.

30. Ibid., 59–61.

31. Congar, *Holy Spirit* 3:157.

32. Robert Murray, *Symbols of Church and Kingdom: A Study in Early Syraic Tradition* (London: Cambridge University Press, 1975), 21–22.

33. Congar, *Holy Spirit* 3:157.

34. Murray, *Symbols of Church and Kingdom*, 22.

35. Pagels, *The Gnostic Gospels*, 67–68. Pagels points out, however, that it was not the thinking of the orthodox Clement which prevailed in the church during the coming centuries. Rather, it was that of Tertullian, who forbade women to speak in church, to teach, to baptize, or to celebrate the eucharist.

36. Congar, *Holy Spirit* 3:157.

37. Ibid., 163.

38. Murray, *Symbols of Church and Kingdom*, 318.

39. Congar, *Holy Spirit* 1:13.

40. Gelpi, *The Divine Mother*, 61–65.

41. Tavard, *Woman in Christian Tradition*, 160–63. For a current reading of sophiology and its application to feminist spirituality, see Cady et al., *Sophia*.

42. Joan Chamberlain Engelsman, *The Feminine Dimension of the Divine* (Philadelphia: Westminster Press, 1979), 106–119.

43. G. B. Harrison, annotator, *Lectionary for Mass, C Cycle* (New York: Pueblo Publishing, 1973), 336.

44. Murray, *Symbols of Church and Kingdom*, 316–19. Also see Congar,

Holy Spirit 3:160–63 where he addresses the issue of the eucharist and the pope as substitutes for the Holy Spirit.

45. Engelsman, *The Feminine Dimension,* 95–106. Moore, "Intermediaries in Jewish Theology," 41–42, further points out that the Old Testament symbols of *Memra, Shekinah,* and *Metatron,* symbols which stand for intermediaries between the divine and the human, were in time subsumed by the intermediary figure of the New Testament, Jesus of Nazareth.

46. Engelsman, *The Feminine Dimension,* 139–48.

47. Congar, *Holy Spirit* 3:156.

48. Engelsman, *The Feminine Dimension,* 133–39.

49. Ibid., 121–33.

50. J. Edgar Bruns, *God as Woman, Woman as God* (New York: Paulist Press, 1973), 66-69.

51. See, e.g., Andrew M. Greeley, *The Mary Myth: On the Femininity of God* (New York: Harper & Row, 1977).

52. Engelsman, *The Feminine Dimension,* 95.

53. Pagels, *The Gnostic Gospels,* 59–67.

54. Engelsman, *The Feminine Dimension,* 139.

55. Ibid., 139–40.

56. Congar, *Holy Spirit* 3:160.

57. Bruns, *God as Woman* (citation taken from the book jacket).

58. Walter Brueggmann, *Theology of Land Conference 1985,* Copyright 1985, National Catholic Rural Life Conference (tape).

59. Ira Chenus, "War and Myth: The Show Must Go On," *Journal of the American Academy of Religion* 53, no. 3 (1985): 449–64. In this article, Chenus argues that the nuclear debate has, in fact, been won at the rational level by the peace activists. However, we still go on planning for total destruction because we are not acting on a rational level, but on a mythological level. Therefore, if peace is to become a reality, what needs to be changed are our myths.

60. Ann Carson, *Feminist Spirituality and the Feminine Divine: An Annotated Bibliography* (Trumansburg, NY: Crossing Press, 1986), 56.

61. Gelpi, *The Divine Mother,* 140.

62. See, e.g., Cady, *Sophia,* esp. 73–75 in regard to some concerns about the use of this symbol, and 80–86 for some positive values that the symbol of *sophia* provides.

63. See Rosemary Radford Ruether, *Women Church: Theology and Practice of Feminist Liturgical Communities* (San Francisco: Harper & Row, 1985), 41–74. Ruether points out that most religions, including Christianity in most of its practices, has functioned to sacralize the social status quo. However, she would see the prophetic tradition in both Judaism and Christianity as standing against this usual picture. Thus the prophets and prophetesses, including Jesus, saw God/ess as the One who sides with the weak and oppressed against those in power. The problem is that this insight of God/ess has never been

applied self-consciously to the bondage of women under patriarchy. It is up
to women to do this, i.e., by the creation of Women Church as a feminist
exodus community.

64. See, e.g., Mary Daly, *Pure Lust: Elemental Feminist Philosophy* (Boston:
Beacon Press, 1984). In this volume, Daly begins to create, through the use
of a new language, a radical feminist world view.

65. Judith Plaskow, "The Right Question Is Theological," in *On Being
a Jewish Feminist,* ed. Heschel, 227–28.

66. Rita M. Gross, "Steps Toward Feminine Imagery of Deity in Jewish
Theology," in *On Being a Jewish Feminist,* ed. Heschel, 245.

67. Ibid., 236.

68. Ibid., 236.

69. Ibid., 237.

70. Ibid., 237.

71. Ibid., 245.

72. Rita M. Gross, "Female God-language in a Jewish Context," in
Womanspirit Rising: A Feminist Reader in Religion, ed. Carol P. Christ and
Judith Plaskow (New York: Harper & Row, 1979), 170–71. Through my great
reluctance to use the term God/ess because of the reaction I knew it would
elicit, I was personally able to share in this experience.

73. It is not clear whether one may assume that the Father is both masculine
and feminine. I am inclined to make this assumption since it is clear that
the Mother is both masculine and feminine.

74. Tavard, *Woman in Christian Tradition,* 163–64. Bulgakov's stand has
been criticized because he takes one attribute (or emanation), Wisdom, and
makes it the whole.

75. Gelpi, *The Divine Mother,* 215–17.

76. Ibid., 216.

77. Ibid., 219–30. Of interest is Gelpi's reasoning for why the Word became
male:

> Moreover, if the preceding reflections enjoy validity, they yield an important insight
> into why God became incarnate as a male. He did so not because men enjoy
> special likeness to God as they sometimes in egotistical arrogance imagine them-
> selves to do, but because in the patriarchal world in which we live males spontane-
> ously tend to align themselves with anti-Christ. God, therefore, became incarnate
> in a male body in order to die in the flesh to patriarchal prejudice and bigotry
> and to teach His disciples, both men and women, to do the same. Anyone, therefore,
> who endorses or acquiesces in sexism stands thereby aligned with the forces
> of anti-Christ. And those who claim divine sanction for sexist social structures
> blaspheme.

78. See, e.g., Mollenkott, *The Divine Feminine.*

79. Marjorie H. Suchocki, *God-Christ-Church: A Practical Approach to
Process Theology,* (New York: Crossroad, 1982), 219–20.

80. See., e.g. Gelpi, *The Divine Mother,* 65, for a contemporary example of this type of theologizing. He would see the function of Jesus as being to teach us who the Holy Spirit (and the Father) is.

81. These three perspectives might be compared to the relationships that could exist between a wife and husband in a marriage. In the first perspective, husband and wife are both independent and dependent—they enjoy both unity and autonomy. In the second model, husband is defined by who the wife is, while in the third model, the wife is defined by who the husband is.

82. This model has its Christian roots in the New Testament where it may be seen, e.g., in John 15:26, where the function of the Holy Spirit is to reveal to us who Christ is.

83. Montague, *The Holy Spirit,* 49–50.

84. Ibid., 70–71. Cf., also, Gen. 1–2.

85. Ibid., 60.

86. Congar, *Holy Spirit* 3:157.

87. Irenaeus, *Against the Heresies* IV, 62.

88. Yves Congar, *Tradition and Traditions* (New York: Macmillan, 1967), 374.

89. Albert Nolan, *Jesus Before Christianity* (Maryknoll, NY: Orbis Books, 1978), 124. For an exposition of the concept of the prophets as those who are in touch with the feeling side of God/ess, see Abraham Heschel, *The Prophets* (New York: Harper & Row, 1962).

90. Montague, *Holy Spirit,* 16–54, passim.

91. Ibid., 326–27.

92. Ibid., 95.

93. Irenaeus, *Against the Heresies* III, xxiv, 1; IV, xx, 5–9.

94. See, e.g., J. H. D. Kelly, *Early Christian Creeds* (New York: David McKay, 1972), 155–66. The earliest known creed, the Old Roman (second half of the second century), specifically relates the Holy Spirit to the church and its teachings of the remission of sins and the resurrection of the flesh. The pattern is common in subsequent creeds and is still to be found in the creeds of the church today.

95. Thomas Hopko, "The Spirit in Orthodox Theology and Life," in *God, Jesus, and Spirit,* ed. Daniel Callahan (New York: Herder and Herder, 1969), 268. Hopko sees the issue between the relationship of authority and the freedom of the Spirit as precisely the issue that divides the Orthodox East from the Roman and Reformed West.

96. Edward O'Connor, "The Spirit in Catholic Thought," in *God, Jesus, Spirit,* ed. Callahan, 246.

97. Edmund J. Fortman, *The Triune God: A Historical Study of the Doctrine of the Trinity* (Philadelphia: Westminister Press, 1972), 243.

98. Cf., e.g., Daniel Maguire, "The Spirit and Church Authority," in *God, Jesus, Spirit,* ed. Callahan, 330–48, for a Catholic view on church authority that puts the Spirit above the church.

99. Albert C. Outler, "Veni, Creator Spiritus: The Doctrine of the Holy
Spirit," in *New Theology, No. 4,* ed. Martin E. Marty and Dean G. Peerman
(New York: Macmillan, 1967), 196.

100. The issues of the church and the world are presented separately, not
because I see them in opposition to one another, but merely as a conventional
way of handling the material.

101. Those who are in the church differ from those who are not in that
we specifically acknowledge that it is through the Holy Spirit that we do what
we do. By our confession we put ourselves in a special position of responsibility
before God/ess for the world.

Chapter Two: Psychological Insights into the Feminine

1. Catherine Keller, *From a Broken Web: Separation, Sexism and Self* (Boston: Beacon Press, 1986), 2.

2. Jean Baker Miller, *Toward a New Psychology of Women* (Boston: Beacon Press, 1976), 7–10.

3. Demaris S. Wehr, *Jung and Feminism: Liberating Archetypes* (Boston: Beacon Press, 1987). "Internalized inferiority" is a phrase used throughout the book.

4. Polly Young-Eisendrath and Florence Wiedemann, *Female Authority: Empowering Women Through Psychotherapy* (New York: Guilford Press, 1987), 2.

5. Miller, *Toward a New Psychology of Women,* 56.

6. Ibid., 95.

7. Carol Gilligan, *In a Different Voice: Psychological Theory and Women's Development* (Cambridge: Harvard University Press, 1982), 13. This perspective in itself is not new to patriarchy. However the validity of women's perceptions is honored and affirmed with fresh insight.

8. Ibid., 19.

9. Ibid., 63.

10. Ibid., 171.

11. Ibid., 173.

12. Nancy Chodorow, *The Reproduction of Mothering: Psychoanalysis and the Sociology of Gender* (Berkeley: University of California Press, 1978), 57.

13. Ibid., 11.

14. Ibid., 219.

15. Keller, *From a Broken Web,* 136.

16. Ibid., 3.

17. Ibid., 106.

18. Ibid., 107–108.

19. C. G. Jung "Psychological Aspects of the Mother Archetype," in *Collected Works* (Princeton: Princeton University Press, 1969) 9:26, cited in Keller, ibid., 112.

20. Keller, *From a Broken Web*, 151.

21. Barbara Dunn, "James Hillman on Soul and Spirit," *The Common Boundary* 6 (1988):8.

22. Barbara Dunn, "The Conscious Feminine," *The Common Boundary*, (1989):12.

23. Emma Jung, *Animus and Anima* (Dallas: Spring Publications, 1985), 28.

24. C. G. Jung, "Two Essays on Analytical Psychology," in *Collected Works*, (Princeton: Princeton University Press, 1972) 7:188.

25. See Toni Wolff, *Structural Forms of the Feminine Psyche* (Zurich: Students Association of the C. G. Jung Institute, 1956) cited in Irene Claremont de Castillejo, *Knowing Woman: A Feminine Psychology* (New York, Harper & Row, 1973), p. 64.

26. Claremont de Castillejo, *Knowing Woman*, 55.

27. Keller, *From a Broken Web*, 116.

28. Emma Jung, *Animus and Anima*, 16.

29. Young-Eisendrath and Wiedemann, *Female Authority*, 20.

30. Sexual relations between therapists and clients are not uncommon and raise ethical questions. In addition,

> if a male analyst has intercourse, or even engages in flirtation, with a female patient he will be playing into her social conditioning to find her worth in her attractiveness to a man. This confirmation of her sexual attractiveness will not help her emerge into full personhood. . .

but encourages her to remain accepting and passive in relations to society's norms, ultimately and confusingly detrimental to her self-esteem. See Wehr, *Jung and Feminism*, 72.

31. C. G. Jung "Psychological Aspects of the Mother Archetype," in *Collected Works* 9:26.

32. Ibid., 17, 28.

33. Ibid., 40.

34. See C. G. Jung, *Collected Works* 10:41, cited in Wehr, *Jung and Feminism*, 65.

35. Edward C. Whitmont, *The Symbolic Quest: Basic Concepts of Analytical Psychology* (Princeton: Princeton University Press, 1969), 201.

36. C. G. Jung, "Two Essays on Analytical Psychology," 7:208.

37. Ibid., 7:209.

38. Wehr, *Jung and Feminism*, 122.

39. Jung has been criticized for his dogmatic approach to both psychology and religion, particularly as regards women and the feminine. In addition to being sexist, Jung has been accused of being racist and classist. See Wehr, *Jung and Feminism*, 75.

40. Ibid., 80–83.

41. Jean Shinoda Bolen, *Goddesses in Everywoman: A New Psychology of Women* (New York: Harper & Row, 1984), 6.

42. Ibid., 20.

43. See n. 41. A book discussing the same topic but from a more personal perspective is the widely acclaimed *The Goddess: Mythological Images of the Feminine* by Christine Downing (New York: Crossroad, 1981).

44. Bolen, *Goddesses in Everywoman,* 14–17.

45. Ibid., 33.

46. Sylvia Brinton Perera, *Descent to the Goddess: A Way of Initiation for Women* (Toronto: Inner City Books, 1981), 36.

47. Ibid., 30.

48. Ibid., 10.

49. Ibid., 7–15.

50. Ibid., 12–30.

51. Ibid., 45.

52. Naomi R. Goldenberg, *Changing of the Gods: Feminism and the End of Traditional Religions* (Boston: Beacon Press, 1979), 75.

53. Erich Neumann, *The Great Mother: An Analysis of the Archetype* (Princeton: Princeton University Press, 1963), 3.

54. C. G. Jung, "Psychological Aspects of the Mother Archetype," 9:42–43.

55. Further exploration of our need to honor the sacred nature of matter can be found in the writings of: Teilhard de Chardin, i.e., *The Divine Milieu* (New York: Harper & Row, 1960); *The Heart of Matter* (New York: Harcourt Brace Jovanovich, 1978); *How I Believe* (New York: Harper & Row, 1969); Brian Swimme, *The Universe is a Green Dragon* (Santa Fe, NM: Bear & Company, 1985); Thomas Berry, *The Dream of the Earth* (San Francisco: Sierra Club Books, 1988); *Thomas Berry and the New Cosmology* (Mystic, CT: Twenty-Third Publications, 1988) as well as through the lectures offered through the Riverdale Center for Religious Research in New York. Thomas Berry is the founder and director. Also, the Teilhard Series of monographs is available to the members of The American Teilhard Association for the Future of Man, Inc., White Plains, NY.

56. C. G. Jung, "A Psychological Approach to the Trinity," in *Collected Works,* 11:36.

57. Ibid., 66–67.

58. For contemporary theological thought regarding the divinity of Mary, see Leonardo Boff, *The Maternal Face of God: The Feminine and its Religious Expressions,* trans. Robert R. Barr and John W. Diercksmeier (San Francisco, Harper & Row, 1987).

59. Jung, "A Psychological Approach to the Trinity," 11:267.

60. Engelsman, *The Feminine Dimension,* 25.

61. Neumann, *The Great Mother,* 59.

62. Ibid., 326.

63. Ibid., 47.

64. Ibid., 62–79.

65. Ibid., 287–88.

66. Ibid., 291–93.

67. Ibid., 331, plates 176–77.

68. Ibid., 332, plate 180.

69. Ibid., 330.

Chapter Three: The Goddess

1. Riane Eisler, *The Chalice and the Blade: Our History, Our Future* (San Francisco: Harper & Row, 1987), 21.

2. Marija Gimbutas, "Women and Culture in Goddess-Oriented Old Europe," in *The Politics of Women's Spirituality: Essays on the Rise of Spiritual Power Within the Feminist Movement* ed. Charlene Spretnak (New York: Anchor Books, 1982), 23.

3. Marija Gimbutas, *The Goddesses and Gods of Old Europe 6500–3500 B.C.: Myths and Cult Images* (Berkeley: University of California Press, 1982), 17.

4. Ibid., 236.

5. Ibid., 152–59.

6. Ibid., 152, 159, 196.

7. Ibid., 176–77.

8. Ibid., 186–87.

9. Ibid., 112.

10. Ibid., 135–45.

11. Ibid., 201–217.

12. Ibid., 227–35.

13. Ibid., 91.

14. Ibid., 237–38.

15. Carol P. Christ, *Laughter of Aphrodite: Reflections on a Journey to the Goddess* (San Francisco: Harper & Row, 1987), 122.

16. Merlin Stone, *Ancient Mirrors of Womanhood: A Treasury of Goddess and Heroing Lore from Around the World* (Boston: Beacon Press, 1984), 73, 31, 140.

17. Marija Gimbutas, "Vulvas, Breasts and Buttocks of the Goddess Creatress: Commentary on the Origins of Art," in *The Shape of the Past: Studies in Honor of Franklin D. Murphy,* ed. Giorgio Buccellati and Charles Speroni (Los Angeles: University of California, Institute of Archaeology, 1981), 8–11. I am tempted to ask whether, if thousands of naked male figurines were discovered, would we assume they were the work of women expressing their erotic experiences or might they represent something else?

18. Merlin Stone, *When God Was a Woman* (New York: Harcourt Brace Jovanovich, 1976), xviii.

19. Charlene Spretnak, *Lost Goddesses of Early Greece: A Collection of Pre-Hellenic Myths* (Boston: Beacon Press, 1978), 22.

20. *Webster's Seventh New Collegiate Dictionary* (Springfield: G. & C. Merriam Co., 1965)

21. Stone, *Ancient Mirrors of Womanhood,* 6–8.

22. Stone, *When God Was a Woman,* 157.

23. Ibid., xx.

24. See Phyllis Trible, *Texts of Terror: Literary-Feminist Readings of Biblical Narratives* (Philadelphia: Fortress Press, 1984).

25. Christ, *Laughter of Aphrodite,* 47, 78–79.

26. See Rita Gross, "Hindu Female Deities as a Resource for the Contemporary Rediscovery of the Goddess," *Journal of the American Academy of Religion* 46, no. 3 (1978): 269–91; and Sarah B. Pomeroy, *Goddesses, Whores, Wives, and Slaves: Women in Classical Antiquity* (New York, Schocken Books, 1975).

27. Margot Adler, *Drawing Down the Moon: Witches, Druids, Goddess-Worshippers, and Other Pagans in America Today* (Boston: Beacon Press, 1986), 190–196.

28. Stone, *When God Was a Woman*, 154.

29. Charlene Spretnak, *The Politics of Women's Spirituality: Essays on the Rise of Spiritual Power Within the Feminist Movement* (New York: Anchor Press, 1982), xii.

30. Stone, *When God Was a Woman*, 59–61.

31. Adrienne Rich, "Prepatriarchal Female Goddess Images," in *The Politics of Women's Spirituality*, ed. Spretnak, 33.

32. Eisler, *The Chalice and the Blade*, 44.

33. Stone, *When God Was a Woman*, 64–66.

34. Eisler, *The Chalice and the Blade*, 45–53.

35. Ibid., 97.

36. Stone, *When God Was a Woman*, 59.

37. Ibid., 161.

38. Stone, *Ancient Mirrors of Womanhood*, 17.

39. Christ, *Laughter of Aphrodite*, 9.

40. Stone, *When God Was a Woman*, 166.

41. See Trible, *Texts of Terror*, passim.

42. See, for example, Judg. 2:13; 3:7; 1 Sam. 7:3–4; Jer. 44:15–19; 2 Kings 17:9.

43. Stone, *When God Was a Woman*, 215.

44. Mary Daly, *Pure Lust: Elemental Feminist Philosophy* (Boston: Beacon Press, 1984), 97–98.

45. Stone, *When God Was a Woman*, 201.

46. Ibid., 218–222.

47. Phyllis Chesler, "The Amazon Legacy," in *The Politics of Women's Spirituality*, ed. Spretnak, 101–102.

48. Pomeroy, *Goddesses, Whores, Wives, and Slaves*, 8–12.

49. Spretnak, *Lost Goddesses of Early Greece*, 18. As explored earlier in chapter 2, the Greek Goddesses can be immensely helpful in identifying various aspects of women's experience. Nevertheless, because of the patriarchial bias evidenced in the storytelling, these Goddesses present mixed messages for women searching for Feminine Divine models. Because each Goddess is identified with specific qualities, to the exclusion of others, there tends to be distortion and imbalance.

50. Stone, *When God Was a Woman*, 133–52.

51. Gerald Massey, *The Natural Genesis*, vol. 2 (New York: Samuel Weiser, 1974), 356.

52. Ibid., 356. Massey also explores the Charis tradition as referred to in Isa. 47:2 (see 365).

53. Penelope Shuttle and Peter Redgrove, *The Wise Wound: Menstruation and Everywoman* (Worcester, MA: The Trinity Press, 1986), 195.

54. Sabrina Sojourner, "From the House of Yemanja: The Goddess Heritage of Black Women," in *The Politics of Women's Spirituality*, ed. Spretnak, 63.

55. Shuttle and Redgrove, *The Wise Wound*, 29.

56. Ibid., 20. We realize that in Scripture Mary Magdalene was not a prostitute. However, since she is still thought of as such by most people, she, along with Mary the mother of Jesus, can metaphorically represent the sexual split that patriarchy has heaped upon women.

57. Georg Groddeck, *The Book of the It* (New York: Mentor, 1961), 95, 154–57.

58. Esther Harding, *Women's Mysteries: Ancient and Modern* (New York: Harper & Row, 1971), 69.

59. Starhawk, *Dreaming the Dark: Magic, Sex and Politics* (Boston: Beacon Press, 1982) pp. 186–87.

60. Shuttle and Redgrove, *The Wise Wound*, 203–204, 211.

61. It is impossible to know the exact number of deaths during the witch burnings. See Shuttle and Redgrove, *The Wise Wound*, 203: "nine million deaths from the date of this Papal Bull [1484 by Pope Innocent VIII] until the end of the seventeenth century"; Eisler *The Chalice and the Blade*, 140: "men sadistically inflicted hideous tortures on many thousands, possibly millions, of 'witches'"; Barbara Walker, *The Crone: Woman of Age, Wisdom, and Power* (San Francisco: Harper & Row, 1985), 142: "About nine million persons were executed after 1484, and uncounted numbers before that date, mostly women"; Matilda Joslyn Gage, *Woman, Church and State*, 2nd ed. (New York: Arno Press, 1972), 247: "It is computed from historical records that nine millions of persons were put to death for witchcraft after 1484"; Felix Morrow's foreword to Montague Summers, *The History of Witchcraft and Demonology* (Secaucus, NJ: Citadel Press, 1971), viii: "The figures of scholars estimating the number of witches put to death vary enormously, from 30,000 to several million"; Rosemary Radford Ruether, *Sexism and God-Talk: Toward a Feminist Theology* (Boston: Beacon Press, 1983), 82: "witch-hunting . . . took the lives of as many as a million people, most of them women."

The issue here, however, is larger than an effort to find the exact number of deaths. We condemn any practice where a woman is killed, tortured, or otherwise debilitated. Mary Daly comments in *Gyn/Ecology*, 183–84:

> The situation of those accused of witchcraft was somewhat different from that of the footbound Chinese girls and of the genitally maimed girls and young women of Africa, for these were mutilated in preparation for their destiny—marriage. It was also somewhat different from the situation of the widows of India, who were killed solely for the crime of outliving their husbands. For the targets of attack in the witchcraze were not women defined by assimilation into the patriarchal family. Rather, the witchcraze focused predominantly upon women who had rejected marriage (Spinsters) and women who had survived it (widows).

62. Starhawk, *Dreaming the Dark*, 187–88.

63. Ibid., 191–204.

64. Ibid., 212–15.

65. Harding, *Women's Mysteries,* 216.

66. Rosemary Radford Ruether, *New Woman, New Earth: Sexist Ideologies & Human Liberation* (New York, Seabury Press, 1975), 105–106.

67. Shuttle and Redgrove, *The Wise Wound,* 218–22.

68. Ibid., 201.

69. Janet and Stewart Farrar, *Eight Sabbats for Witches* (London: Robert Hale, 1981), 12.

70. Starhawk, *The Spiral Dance: A Rebirth of the Ancient Religion of the Great Goddess* (San Francisco: Harper & Row, 1979), 35–37.

71. Starhawk, *Dreaming the Dark,* 9–11.

72. Jane Ellen Harrison, *Prolegomena to the Study of Greek Religion from Ancient Religion and Mythology* (New York: Arno Press, 1975), 286.

73. Harding, *Women's Mysteries,* 111.

74. Janet and Stewart Farrar, *The Witches' Goddess: The Feminine Principle of Divinity* (Washington, DC: Phoenix, 1987), 35–36.

75. Walker, *The Crone,* 72, 85.

76. Farrar, *Eight Sabbats for Witches,* 13–23.

77. Starhawk, *The Spiral Dance,* 110–43.

78. Ibid., 84–101.

Chapter Four: The Christian Trinity and the Feminine Divine

1. June Singer, *Androgyny: Toward a New Theory of Sexuality* (Garden City, NY: Doubleday, 1976), 20.

2. Ibid., 34.

3. Consult Singer's *Androgyny,* which explicates the meaning of androgyny in the various traditions to which this sentence refers.

4. Rosemary Radford Ruether, *Sexism and God-Talk: Toward a Feminist Theology* (Boston: Beacon Press, 1983), 52, also notes that the concept of gender complementarity is absent from the ancient Goddess texts (2800-1200 B.C.). Rather, the Gods and Goddesses are seen as equivalent. Thus, for example, Ishtar is seen, not as the embodiment of so-called feminine qualities, such as nurturance, but "as the expression of divine sovereignty and power in female form."

5. See Judith Ochshorn, *The Female Experience and the Nature of the Divine* (Bloomington, IN: Indiana University Press, 1981). It must be noted that while this androgynous religious milieu was good for priestesses, it was not beneficent for women in general. The implications of this for our contemporary experience of an ordained class of people deserve consideration.

6. See, Carolyn G. Heilbrun, *Toward a Recognition of Androgyny* (New York: Knopf, 1964). Heilbrun treats specifically of the literary issue.

7. Ibid., 170.

8. See, e.g., Elizabeth A. Johnson, "The Incomprehensibility of God and the Image of God Male and Female," *Theological Studies* 45 (1984) 441–65. This article is particularly valuable in that it offers a critique of what Johnson considers to be the three ways in which theology today deals with the issue

of imaging God as female as well as male. These are (1) to attribute "feminine" qualities to a God who is basically understood as a masculine person, (2) to uncover a feminine dimension in God, which dimension is usually realized in the person of the Holy Spirit, and (3) to image God according to the fullness of humanity, which is equivalently both male and female.

While Johnson's presentation is insightful, I would not agree with her assessment of the Holy Spirit as being too mysterious (458) and too stereotypically feminine (459–60). The former argument would be contradicted by, for example, Leonardo Boff, *The Maternal Face of God* (San Francisco: Harper & Row, 1987), while the latter would be contradicted by such images of the Spirit as Wisdom and Creativity.

9. R. M. Gross, "Steps Toward Feminine Imaging of Deity in Jewish Theology," in *On Being a Jewish Feminist: A Reader,* ed. Susannah Heschel (New York: Schocken Books, 1983), 236–37.

10. Carol Ochs, *Behind the Sex of God: Toward a New Consciousness—Transcending Matriarchy and Patriarchy* (Boston: Beacon Press, 1977), 82–109.

11. See, e.g., Catherine Keller, *From a Broken Web: Separation, Sexism, and Self* (Boston: Beacon Press, 1986), 12–18.

12. Joseph A. Bracken, *What Are They Saying About the Trinity?* (New York: Paulist Press, 1979), 78.

13. Ibid., 78–79. However, Bracken hesitates to say whether one should break out of the family model which tradition has used so frequently. Nonetheless, he does state that if Christian dogma is to speak authentically to women and men today, it must be reinterpreted along bisexual, communitarian, processive lines.

14. Jürgen Moltmann, *The Trinity and the Kingdom: The Doctrine of God* (San Francisco: Harper & Row, 1981), 60–96.

15. Ibid., 94.

16. Ibid., 95. Moltmann develops two additional models (97–128) based on the Trinity's relationship to creation. Thus, in the outpouring of the Holy Spirit, the divine order is the procession of the Spirit from the Father through the Son, whereas in the glorification which the Spirit brings about, the procession is from the Spirit, through the Son, to the Father (Eph. 1:18), a reversal of the first order.

17. Jürgen Moltmann, "The Motherly Father. Is Trinitarian Patripassianism Replacing Theological Patriarchalism?" in *God as Father?*, ed. Johannes-Baptist Metz and Edward Schillebeeckx (Edinburgh: T. & T. Clark, 1981), 53.

18. Ibid., 53.

19. See, e.g., E. Clark and H. Richardson, eds., *Women and Religion* (New York: Harper & Row, 1977), 164–65. Richardson offers the observation that he was taught to say his bedtime prayer to Father-Mother God. Thus he came to understand that God must be different from anything else he had ever experienced.

20. Johnson, "The Incomprehensibility of God," 462.

21. Joseph Fitzmyer, *A Wandering Aramean* (Missoula, MT: Scholars Press, 1979), 134–35.

22. Madeleine Boucher, "The Image of God in the Gospels: Toward a Reassessment" (Unpublished address to the Catholic Biblical Association, August 1984).

23. G. F. Moore, *Judaism* 2 (Cambridge: Harvard University Press, 1950), 211.

24. H. Paul Santmire "Retranslating 'Our Father': the Urgency and the Possibility," *Dialog* 16 (1977): 101–6.

25. Gail Ramshaw Schmidt, "De Divinis Nominibus: The Gender of God," *Worship* 56 (1982): 117.

26. Johnson, "The Incomprehensibility of God," passim.

27. Mary Daly, *Beyond God the Father: Toward a Philosophy of Woman's Liberation* (Boston: Beacon Press, 1973), 8.

28. Ibid., 8.

29. Maynard Kaufman, "Post-Christian Aspects of the Radical Theology" in *Toward a New Christianity: Readings in the Death of God Theology*, ed., Thomas J. J. Altizer (New York: Harcourt, Brace & World, 1967), 361–62.

30. Michael O'Carroll, *Trinitas: A Theological Encyclopedia of the Holy Spirit* (Wilmington, DE: Michael Glazier, 1987), 108.

31. Moltmann, *The Trinity*, 178.

32. O'Carroll, *Trinitas*, 110.

33. Moltmann, *The Trinity*, 166–67.

34. Ibid., 180–81.

35. Ibid., 181.

36. *Origins* (National Catholic News Service) 17, no. 44 (1988): 748–49.

37. Jay G. Williams, "Yahweh, Women and the Trinity," *Theology Today* 32 (1975): 240.

38. Marjorie Hewitt Suchocki, *God-Christ-Church: A Practical Guide to Process Theology* (New York: Crossroad, 1982), 49.

39. Ibid., 55–89.

40. Ibid., 45.

41. Ibid., 103.

42. Ibid., 225.

43. Ibid., 103.

44. Ibid., 213.

45. Ibid., 123–60.

46. Ibid., 76.

47. Ibid., 76.

48. Ibid., 62. However, it should be noted that the very constancy of God/ess as Presence would act to hide her from consciousness. This occurs because "there is no contrasting absence whereby God's presence could rise to conscious notice."

49. Ibid., 93–121.

50. Ibid., 62.

51. Ibid., 62.

52. Ibid., 82–83.

53. Ibid., 163–210.

54. Ibid., 83–87.

55. Ibid., 218–20.

56. See, e.g., Wendy Martyna, "What Does 'She' Mean," *Journal of Communications* 28, no. 1 (1978) for a study that indicates that sex-neutral language does not include women. For the male, sex-neutral language elucidates a male like themselves, while for women, sex-neutral language leaves them imageless.

57. An outstanding exception to the traditional Father-Son-Spirit trinitarian language is Heribert Muhlen, who has written extensively and speaks of the Father as I, the Son as Thou, and the Spirit as We.

58. Mary Collins, "Naming God in Public Prayer," *Worship* 59 (1985): 299.

59. Ibid., 297–98.

60. Miriam Therese Winter, *An Anthology of Scripture Songs* (Philadelphia: Medical Mission Sisters, 1982), 10.

61. Samuel Rayan, "Naming the Unnamable," in *Naming God*, ed. Robert P. Scharlemann (New York: Paragon House, 1985), 10–11.

62. Daly, *Beyond God the Father*, 33.

63. Ibid., 13–44.

64. Leonardo Boff, *The Maternal Face of God: The Feminine and Its Religious Expressions*, trans. Robert R. Barr and John W. Diercksmeier (San Francisco: Harper & Row, 1987).

65. "The Message of the Myth," 2nd program in the PBS television series "Joseph Campbell and the Power of Myth: With Bill Moyers," 1988. The eighth-century carving referred to may be found in a cave on an island in the harbor of Bombay. The center image represents the mask of eternity while the profiled images represent the temporal opposites such as male-female, evil-good, death-life, etc.

66. O'Carroll, *Trinitas*, 129.

67. *Webster's New Universal Unabridged Dictionary*, (New York: Dorset and Baber, 1979).

68. Daly, *Beyond God the Father*, 33.

69. Gelpi, *The Divine Mother*, 140.

Chapter Five: The Feminist Mystic/Prophet

1. Evelyn Underhill, *Mysticism* (New York: Dutton, 1961), 331.

2. Ibid., 414.

3. Walter Brueggemann, *The Prophetic Imagination* (Philadelphia: Fortress, 1978), 59.

4. Ibid., 45.

5. Ibid., 60.

6. Ibid., 62.

7. Rosemary Radford Ruether, *Sexism and God-Talk* (Boston: Beacon Press, 1983), 24.

8. Ibid., 32.

9. Judith Plaskow, "The Coming of Lilith: Toward a Feminist Theology," in *Womanspirit Rising* ed., Christ and Plaskow, 203.

10. Paula Cooey, "The Power of Transformation and the Transformation of Power," *Journal of Feminist Studies in Religion* 1 (1985): 30.

11. Rosemary Radford Ruether, "Motherearth and the Megamachine: A Theology of Liberation in a Feminine, Somatic and Ecological Perspective," in *Womanspirit Rising*, ed., Christ and Plaskow, 52.

12. Christ and Plaskow, eds., *Womanspirit Rising*, 5.

13. Ibid., 5.

14. The discussion of rape is beyond the scope of this presentation. However, recent studies question the justice afforded women who are perceived by society to be sexually promiscuous and thus "deserving" to be raped. How this attitude affects the emotionally disturbed is beyond calculation.

15. Dorothee Soelle, *Strength of the Weak* (Philadelphia: Westminster, 1984), 90.

16. Eleanor L. Mc Laughlin, "The Christian Past: Does It Hold a Future for Women?" in *Womanspirit Rising*, ed., Christ and Plaskow, 96.

17. Brendan Doyle, *Meditations with Julian of Norwich* (Sante Fe, NM: Bear & Company, 1985), 6–8.

18. Ibid., 14.

19. *Julian of Norwich, "Showings,"* ed. Edmund Colledge et al. (New York: Paulist, 1978) 10.

20. Ibid., 293–99.

21. Ruether, *Sexism and God-Talk*, 128–29.

22. Michael Mott, "Thomas Merton: Activist Monk" (Lecture cosponsored by Wainwright House, Rye, NY, and Manhattanville College, Purchase, NY, 8 October 1986).

23. Barbara Mitchell, "Tales from the Gender-Exclusive Woods," *Open* (December, 1986).

24. Lucy Menzies, *The Revelations of Mechthild of Magdeburg* (New York: Longmans, Green & Co., 1953), xxxi.

25. Ibid., 117.

26. Ibid., 173.

27. Ibid., 129.

28. Ibid., 11.

29. Pierre Teilhard de Chardin, *The Heart of Matter* (New York: Harcourt Brace Jovanovich, 1978), 16.

30. Meinrad Craighead, "Immanent Mother," in *The Feminist Mystic*, ed., Mary E. Giles, (New York: Crossroad, 1982), 80.

31. Sue Woodruff, *Meditations with Mechtild of Magdeburg* (Sante Fe, NM: Bear & Company, 1982), 116–17.

32. Matthew Fox, *Breakthrough* (New York: Image Books, 1980), 59.

33. Ibid., sermon 22, 313–24.

34. Ibid., sermon 2, 65–75.

35. Ibid., sermon 14, 199–202.

36. Ibid., 313.

37. Matthew Fox, *Meditations with Meister Eckhart* (Santa Fe, NM: Bear & Company, 1983), 92.

38. Ibid., 105.

39. Fox, *Breakthrough,* 315.

40. Ibid., 499–500.

41. Gabriele Uhlein, *Meditations with Hildegard of Bingen* (Santa Fe, NM: Bear & Company, 1985), 35.

42. Bruce Hozeski, *Hildegard of Bingen's Scivias* (Santa Fe, NM: Bear & Company, 1986), 82.

43. Ibid., 20.

44. Matthew Fox, *Illuminations of Hildegard of Bingen* (Santa Fe, NM: Bear & Company, 1986), 24.

45. Ibid., 32.

46. Hozeski, *Hildegard of Bingen's Scivias,* 183.

Chapter Six: What Was, What Is, What Will Be

1. Thomas Berry, *The Dream of the Earth* (San Francisco: Sierra Club Books, 1988), 138–39.

2. Ibid., 140.

3. Ibid., 140.

4. Riane Eisler, *The Chalice and the Blade* (San Francisco: Harper & Row, 1987), 13–14. The evidence is based on findings in Old Europe (lands extending from the Aegean and Adriatic (including the islands) to Czechoslovakia, southern Poland, and the western Ukraine, as well as to Catal Huyuk and Hacilar in present-day Turkey), 12–14.

5. Ibid., xvi–xvii.

6. Ibid., 29–41. To see how this value is negated in our present-day reality, see, e.g., J. Bryan Hehir, "Third World Debt and the Poor," *Origins* (National Catholic News Service) 18, no. 36 (1989): 607–12, in which Hehir demonstrates how the monies lent to the third world have ultimately benefitted the rich while the poor become ever poorer.

7. Merlin Stone, *When God Was a Woman* (New York: Dial Press, 1976), xxiv.

8. Marija Gimbutas. *The Goddess and Gods of Old Europe, 6500–3500 B.C., Myths and Cult Images* (Berkeley: University of California Press, 1982), Introduction.

9. Stone, *When God Was a Woman,* xii.

10. Ibid., 22. Stone notes that She was revered under many names and titles, such as Celestial Ruler, Sovereign of the Heavens, Her Holiness, Queen of Heaven, Lioness of the Sacred Assembly, Lady of the High Place. However, despite the diversity of language and titles, Stone contends that they refer not to many beings, but to the one Great Goddess.

11. Eisler, *The Chalice and the Blade,* xxiii.

12. Sheila D. Collins, *A Different Heaven and Earth* (Valley Forge: Judson

Press, 1974), 161. The exploitation of woman may be paradigmatic because of the common view of God as male. For if God is male, woman is by definition "other," while at the same time she is biologically and psychologically man's intimate. This ambiguous state of need for that which is other, produces self-hatred in the male, which he projects unto the female. This contradictory state of otherness and intimacy does not exist in regard to males of other classes to the same degree (who are thought of as being in God's image) or in regard to the earth (toward which no need for intimacy is felt).

13. Berry, *The Dream of the Earth*, 145–59.

14. Ibid., 145.

15. Collins, *Different Heaven and Earth*, 154–57.

16. Berry, *The Dream of the Earth*, 143.

17. For a well-documented exposition of patriarchy as an historical process, see Gerda Lerner, *The Creation of Patriarchy* (New York: Oxford University Press, 1986).

18. Ibid., 238. Lerner defines sex as that which distinguishes women as "a separate group due to their biological distinctiveness" whereas "gender is the cultural definition of behavior defined as appropriate to the sexes in a given society at a given time."

19. David P. Barash and Judith Eve Lipton, *The Caveman and the Bomb: Human Nature, Evolution, and Nuclear War* (New York: McGraw-Hill, 1985), 250.

20. Ibid., 249–51. Based on this biological factor, Barash and Lipton see the need to encourage "mothering men" who can celebrate life as women do.

21. Elizabeth Dodson Gray, *Green Paradise Lost* (Wellesley, MA: Roundtable Press, 1979), 49. See, e.g., the PBS television series "Joseph Campbell and the Power of Myth," 1988, which concentrates on the male heroic journey as the quintessential human "male" experience.

22. Lerner, *The Creation of Patriarchy*, 217.

23. Ibid., 220–21.

24. Berry, *The Dream of the Earth*, 149.

25. Ibid., 158–59. This would call for a new American dream or vision, since the current American dream may be equated with the destruction of the natural world through the construction of shopping malls, highways, corporate headquarters, airports, etc. (156).

26. One of the most powerful expositions on the relationship between women and the land was that given by Walter Brueggmann at the *Theology of Land Conference 1985*, sponsored by the National Catholic Rural Life Conference (available on audio tape from the Conference). In this talk Brueggmann described the parallel that exists in American history between the treatment of land and the treatment of women. Both are exploited as objects of production/reproduction. The treatment of both women and the land is traditionally either one of promiscuity (they are used and then discarded when no longer useful) or of domination (they are held tightly until the life is squeezed out of them). Brueggmann calls men to a relationship of loyalty and freedom with both the

land and women, a relationship of partnership instead of possession. Because of the interconnection between the economic and the sexual, he thinks that we will not have a new land ethic until we have a new sexual ethic; he sees them as intricately related.

27. Val Plumwood, "Ecofeminism: An Overview and Discussion of Positions and Arguments," in *Women and Philosophy,* ed. Janna L. Thompson (*Australian Journal of Philosophy,* supplement to vol. 64, 1986), 120.

28. Lynn White, Jr., "The Historical Roots of our Ecologic Crisis," *Science* 155 (1967): 1205.

29. Ibid., 1205

30. Ibid., 1205

31. Ibid., 1207.

32. Ibid., 1207. White proposes Francis of Assisi, who understood the equality of all of God's creatures, as the key to the solution of the crisis (1206–1207).

33. Rosemary Radford Ruether, *New Woman, New Earth* (New York: Seabury Press, 1975), 194–95.

34. Ibid., 194–96.

35. Ibid., 202. Ruether suggests that, rather than dealing with the needed systemic changes, business and government will peddle "ecological band-aids" aimed at the already overfragmented housewife. The housewife may turn to these to placate her conscience, and thereby do more and more to accomplish less and less. In the meantime, the real ecological problems—which rest with industry—will continue unimpeded (200–201).

36. Ruether, *Sexism and God-Talk,* 259. Ruether's treatment of dualism is theological. For a nontheological treatment that ranges through a wide spectrum of Western disciples, see Susan Griffin, *Woman and Nature: The Roaring Inside Her* (New York: Harper Colophon Books, 1978).

37. Carolyn Merchant, *The Death of Nature: Ecology and the Scientific Revolution* (San Francisco: Harper & Row, 1983), xv–xvi.

38. Ibid., xvii.

39. Ibid., 2.

40. Ibid., xvi.

41. Ibid., 3.

42. Ibid., 3.

43. Ibid., 164–73.

44. Ibid., 190–92. (For the articulation of this idea, see 192–236.)

45. Ibid., 238.

46. Mary Daly, *Beyond God the Father: Toward a Philosophy of Women's Liberation* (Boston: Beacon Press, 1973), 178.

47. Ibid., 178.

48. Ibid., 178.

49. Gray, *Green Paradise Lost,* 10–11.

50. Ibid., 121.

51. Diane LeBow, "Rethinking Matriliny Among the Hopi," in *Women in Search of Utopia,* ed. Ruby Rohrlich and Elaine Hoffman Baruch (New York: Schocken Books, 1984), 8–20. In this article on gender differentiation, LeBow

argues, based on her analysis of the Hopi culture, that an equality of difference can actually exist. Much more work needs to be done in this disputed area. For a further work of note, see Eleanor Burke Leacock, *Myths of Male Dominance: Collected Articles on Women Cross-Culturally* (New York: Monthly Review Press, 1981).

52. It was interesting to hear the response of a woman religious who was recently asked, Whatever happened to the nuns to cause them to change so radically? She responded, "Why, we did exactly what Rome told us to do. We read the Gospels for the first time."

53. Ruether, *Sexism and God-Talk*, 214.

54. Ibid., 214–16.

55. Daly, *Beyond God the Father*, 157.

56. A certain amount of ambiguity is contained in the literature on the unity of the personal and the political. The writers appear to be speaking in terms of the personal and the political as a relationship of the one and the many. Furthermore, the spiritual seems to be equated with the category of the one. Deeper reflection and dialogue is needed to bring clarity to this critical issue.

57. Dorothy I. Riddle, "Politics, Spirituality, and Models of Change," in *The Politics of Women's Spirituality,* ed. Charlene Spretnak (Garden City, NY: Anchor Books, 1982), 374–75.

58. Charlene Spretnak, "The Unity of Politics and Spirituality," in *The Politics of Women's Spirituality,* 350.

59. Ibid., 351.

60. Hallie Iglehart, "The Unnatural Divorce of Spirituality and Politics," in *The Politics of Women's Spirituality,* ed. Spretnak, 413.

61. Ibid.

62. Judith Antonelli, "Feminist Spirituality: The Politics of the Psyche," in *The Politics of Women's Spirituality,* ed. Spretnak, 399.

63. Ibid., 402.

64. Baba Copper, "The Voice of Women's Spirituality in Futurism" in *The Politics of Women's Spirituality,* ed. Spretnak, 508.

65. See, e.g., Berry, *The Dream of the Earth*, 43, for a view that refutes the possibility of reformation. Berry says, "Our problems can no more be resolved within our former pattern of the human than the problems that led to quantum physics could be dealt with by any adjustment within the contest of the Newtonian universe."

66. Ruether, *Sexism and God-Talk*, 216–28.

67. Berry, *The Dream of the Earth*, 123–37.

68. Ibid., 80–82. The author would see a need, if our future vision is to become a reality, to think of the earth as part of the cosmos, not as a self-contained entity.

69. Ibid., 43. Signs that this is already taking place may be seen in the demand for environmental impact statements and in the United Nations World Charter for Nature, approved by the Assembly in 1982.

70. This mandate is given to the Christian when s/he is told: "And he

said to them: Go into all the world and preach the gospel to the whole creation" (Mark 16:15).

71. Berry, *The Dream of the Earth,* xiii.

72. See, e.g., Pat Fleming and Joanna Macy, "The Council of All Beings," in *Thinking Like a Mountain* (Philadelphia: New Society Publishers, 1988), 78–90.

73. Carol S. Pearson, "Of Time and Revolution: Theories of Social Change in Contemporary Feminist Science Fiction", in *Women in Search of Utopia,* ed. Ruby Rohrlich and Elaine Hoffman Baruch (New York: Schocken Books, 1984), 268.

Index

153